MW01138938

COUNTER WOKECRAFT

A Field Manual for Combatting the Woke
in the University and Beyond

Charles Pincourt with James Lindsay

New Discourses

First edition: November 2021
Cover copyright © 2021 New Discourses, LLC.

Charles Pincourt with James Lindsay
Counter Wokecraft: A Field Manual for Combatting the Woke in the University and Beyond

ISBN: 9798536815038
Imprint: Independently published

Printed in the United States of America
New Discourses, Orlando, FL
https://newdiscourses.com

Contents

i

iv

Acknowledgements

As I wrote the blogposts that eventually became this book, I received comments and support from a number of people whom I'd like to acknowledge here. Dorian Abbot from the University of Chicago was full of ideas about how to enable dissent from the Critical Social Justice perspective in universities, and I've included several of them in the book. Lee Jussim from Rutgers University and Pedro Domingos at the University of Washington provided input about Woke bullying tactics and were kind enough to tweet out my posts. Similarly, "A Foreign Professor" (@weowethedead on Twitter) gave me good suggestions about formalizing decision-making and was a frequent supporter of the project. Naturally, I was delighted that James Lindsay at New Discourses was inspired by the project and agreed to contribute to, and participate in, the book.

Foreword by James Lindsay

Western Civilization is being ideologically colonized. In fact, it nearly has been ideologically colonized, and only now, at this late stage in the process, are people waking up to the fact. A vast ideological movement has crept in and taken control of most of our societies' noblest and most vital institutions, certainly not least among them education and the universities. People in almost every sector of life often feel paralyzed and helpless now that this ideology is activating itself and wielding its captured institutional power.

Giving a right name for this ideology has been difficult, though a term derived from their own literature—Critical Social Justice—is probably most accurate (while the highly academic term critical constructivism is most precise). Most of us, however, use a slang term it used to use for itself: Woke. The term "Woke" refers to being "awakened" or "woke up" to the alleged realities of "systemic power dynamics" that order society. These alleged power dynamics are said to create what sociologists call "stratifications" in society, like kinds of upper and lower classes, depending on who has "privilege" and who is "oppressed" by various power dynamics like systemic racism (or white supremacy), systemic sexism (or patriarchy or misogyny), cis-heteronormativity, and so on. A certain unreality attends these arguments too, as these power dynamics are often described using dense technical jargon and making use of words in ways that seem at least slightly distorted from their original intended meanings. The Marxian flavor of this analysis—which sees them as structural and sites of necessary conflict—is also obvious but hard to pin down.

Because the Woke ideology, as it will be referred to here, seems to have erupted out of the ground in the last few years, most people are also unaware of the fact that it has, depending on how one counts it, a one- or two-hundred-year-long history and trajectory in aiming to topple the organizational system of liberal Western societies. If nothing else, the deliberate strategy to colonize and change institutions from within, and then to wield them against the society that produced them, has been the strategy since the 1920s, when the Albanian-Italian Communist theorist Antonio Gramsci started laying out the ideas that were in the 1960s named "the long march through the institutions" (by another Marxist thinker, Rudi Dutschke). That is, most people, including those waking up to the reality of this ideological takeover, remain dangerously unaware that the Woke ideology is the culmination of a long-running set of plans that is finally, in these last few years, bearing fruit, mostly through its quiet seizure of institutional power.

Seeing as the Woke ideology is based upon strategic plans developed, tested, and systematically employed over at least a century, it must be acknowledged and understood that it has tactics, particularly for quietly insinuating itself into institutions and taking them over from within. These tactics, which include subtle and strategic manipulations of language and occupying positions of influence and policymaking, can rightly be referred to as Wokecraft, much in the same way that espionage makes use of tools and tactics we would identify as "spycraft." The good news is, these tactics, while tricky and manipulative, are comprehensible, predictable, and able to be countered, and this guide, put together by Charles Pincourt with my assistance is an invaluable contribution to understanding, recognizing, and ultimately countering Wokecraft wherever it rears its head, especially in centers of institutional power.

Pincourt is an academic, and his context is the university, so this useful field manual is tailored to that institution, where administrative hierarchies, policies, and committees rule the roost. The lessons contained within this short volume readily generalize, however, and are applicable throughout life anywhere corporate, administrative, or other bureaucratic policy might be relevant—government, primary and secondary education, the corporate world, churches, and even formal affinity and hobby groups. This makes this field manual a much-needed contribution at this time when people are ready and eager to push back against the Woke ideology by every legal means.

In the first chapter, you will find a useful, clear description of the Woke ideology, including how it thinks about the world. This will help you understand the Woke ideology sufficiently to be able to identify what it is and why it does what it does. From there, a thorough description of many of the tactics of Wokecraft in administrative settings is provided in the second chapter. Readers will be equipped to recognize (and resist) the manipulative tactics of Wokecraft in real time and thus be armed to push back or stop them. In the third chapter, counter-strategies are offered that will enable you to prevent further infection by the Woke ideology and to regain institutional ground where it has already been taken by the Woke. In all, this work is readable, straightforward, and profoundly useful in the prevailing state of affairs in Western societies.

It is my hope, and Charles's, that this short, accessible volume will find its way into as many hands as possible and will prove useful to decolonizing our institutions, which is to say to remove Woke ideology and the influences of Wokecraft from them, effectively and quickly, and to reestablish liberal values in their place. For those of you looking to understand the Woke ideology—Critical Social Justice—better and to take action against it, this is the guide for you.

James Lindsay
July 2021

Introduction

I'm a professor at a large North American university. I'm writing this manual under the pen name Charles Pincourt. I am writing because I am dismayed about the state of North American universities. I'd like to help people understand what is wrong with them and if they are academics, how they can try to change them. I started a blog in October of 2020. This manual is a compilation and reworking of my blog posts from when I started until April 2021. The purpose of the manual is to help those who are concerned about the perspective, but who are not very familiar with it; those who understand that something is wrong, but don't have the background to understand and resist the Critical Social Justice perspective takeover of our universities.

It is designed, at this stage, for academics in an academic environment, although I believe much can be transferred to other work environments. That James Lindsay was willing to contribute to, and support, this book shows he sees the relevance of the book outside of academia as well. I focus on academic environments because that is what I know. The book draws on a great deal of research into the Critical Social Justice perspective and movement. It also draws on my experience in academia and how I have seen Critical Social Justice proponents advance their cause within the academy.

The goal is to help those concerned to understand the CSJ perspective, what drives it, identify when and how it makes inroads, and how to resist and prevent it from taking over your department, faculty or university. Many would say it is too late. While there have been many inroads, the takeover until now has been largely in the fine arts, the humanities and most of the social sciences. While rolling it back may be difficult in these disciplines, it is not too late to protect the sciences, engineering and business schools.

Chapter 1

Understanding Woke

1.1   What is Woke?

Woke is a term given both to a worldview and to the people who are initiated, and adhere, to that worldview. The worldview is known under several pseudonyms: the Critical Perspective, Social Justice and the Critical Social Justice (CSJ) perspective. It is described in Section 1.2 below. It is an amalgam of postmodern and critical theory. The term "Woke" is the simple past of the verb to wake, and it is intended to mean "awoken" to the CSJ worldview.

While the term derives from the CSJ perspective and is used proudly as a self-identifying moniker, the same term is used pejoratively among those critical of the perspective. It is because of its pejorative connotations that I'm reluctant to use it. At the same time, it is difficult to come up with another term that is so understandable and concise. As such, and even though I am reluctant to use pejorative terms, I use the term throughout this book. The definition I'll use for "the Woke" is: people who are conscious of the Critical Social Justice perspective and who adhere to it.

1.2 The Woke Worldview

The Woke worldview actually encompasses a number of different theories relating to inequality between different groups in society. As such, the term includes Critical Race Theory, Queer Theory, Post-colonial Theory and Fat Studies to name a few of the main ones. The key difference between the various approaches to Critical Social Justice really has to do with which group the theories concentrate on. Critical Race Theory emphasizes blacks, Queer Theory emphasizes non-cisgendered people, Post-colonial Theory emphasizes colonized or previously colonized peoples, etc.

The Critical Social Justice (Woke) literature is enormous. The vast majority of that literature is very technical, so that even general books (e.g. Best (1991)) on the topic are very dense and difficult to access for an uninitiated reader. Moreover, most work that is written on the topic is written by people within academia adhering to the perspective, making it difficult to have an objective understanding of it. There have been a few recent attempts to describe the Critical Social Justice perspective from outside of the perspective (but in academia) (e.g. Hicks (2011)) and from outside of the perspective and outside academia (e.g. Pluckrose and Lindsay (2020)). I have found *Cynical Theories* to be the best I have come across, primarily due to its ability to aggregate the various strains of Critical Social Justice as well as to undertake a meta-analysis extracting the key elements that bind the strains together. As a result, I use (and adapt) Pluckrose and Lindsay's framework for understanding the Woke worldview.

So what is the Woke perspective? Ultimately, there are three main principles that bind the many different flavors of Woke together: the knowledge principle, the political principle and the subject principle. The first two principles were coined by Pluckrose & Lindsay in Cynical Theories. I have coined the third (Pincourt; 2021b).

There a few important elements to the knowledge principle. The first is that while reality itself is not denied or questioned, it is considered impossible for us to know its true nature. The reason it's impossible for us to know about reality's true nature is that any knowledge we think we have is actually only "socially constructed;" defined (through language) by the culture in which we live. Critical for this principle is the fact that different cultures have different understandings about the nature of the world. After examining the political principle, the importance of this last point will be clearer.

The political principle is that not only is knowledge socially constructed, but knowledge is constructed by oppressor groups in society at the expense of oppressed groups. The construction of knowledge is done through language whose rules are also determined by groups with the power to do so, i.e. oppressor groups. Moreover, knowledge is constructed in such a way that it helps maintain the oppressive role for oppressor groups and to prevent oppressed groups being liberated from their oppression.

This is taken to imply that not only is any knowledge socially constructed, but it is by definition biased and can't be an accurate representation of reality. This, together with the fact that different cultures have different understandings of the nature of the world, implies that no worldview is more authoritative than any other. As such, all worldviews are (epistemically) equivalent in terms of their ability to know anything about reality, and amount simply to different "stories" about reality. So, for example, the scientific worldview has no greater claim to understanding reality than any other "story." That is, a scientific worldview is no truer than a religious worldview, or even than a superstitious worldview. Moreover the scientific worldview (developed by white, European males) constructs knowledge about reality in such a way as to perpetuate systems of oppression that benefit oppressor white, European males. As such, even the tools used to understand the world according to the scientific worldview such as logic, argument, evidence, hypotheses, controlled experiments, etc. serve to perpetuate oppression.

The subject principle (Pincourt; 2021b) is that individuals are primarily defined by their group identity (white, female, black, European, cis-gendered, etc.). That is to say that they are subjected to their group identity in society - which is why I call this the subject principle (this is how the poststructuralists a.k.a the (high-) postmodernists often referred to individuals, i.e. as subjects). This implies that people are oppressors or oppressed according to what group/groups they are identified with. Similarly, it implies that how people behave is primarily a function of group identity, and (taken together with the political principle) that their behavior supports and helps perpetuate the oppressive systems around them unconsciously. White people for example, simply can't help but behave in ways that perpetuate their oppression over non-white people in society. Importantly, it also implies black people behave in such a way that perpetuates their oppression, although from a different perspective, and that is one reason they behave differently than white people.

A corollary of this principle is that since individual behavior is defined by one's identity, individuals are responsible or accountable for actions associated with any identity to which they are associated. As such, the oppressive acts of one member of a group is the oppressive act of all members of that group. Finally, this accountability is valid across time. The oppressive act of a member of a group at one time can be attributed to a group identity (and its members) at another time.

Taken together we can infer that according to the Woke worldview, reality, well...sucks. We have a reality that is inhabited by individual subjects with little personal autonomy driven to behave according to their group identities. The groups and their constituent subjects are either oppressors or oppressed and everyone consciously or unconsciously behaves to perpetuate the patterns of oppression - yikes!

1.3   The Woke Ethos

Understanding the advance of the Critical Social Justice (CSJ) perspective in North American universities is difficult without understanding the ethos (guiding beliefs) of the Woke. The ethos is closely tied to the Woke Worldview. If one adheres to the grim Woke worldview, and if in addition one is particularly sensitive to care/harm moral foundations (see Haidt (2012)); a characteristic of those on the political left, ethics naturally turn towards the opposition of oppression.

Given (according to CSJ) that oppression and oppressive structures permeate our entire existence, there are many opportunities to oppose oppression. Not only are there many opportunities to do so, but an important aspect of the ethos is that one ought to actively oppose. More recently, that one ought to oppose oppression has been replaced with the notion that if you don't oppose, you are complicit in oppression.

It is difficult to overestimate the zeal and fanaticism of this movement in universities. The zeal of the movement, the moral necessity to oppose oppression, and the radical epistemic skepticism and relativity have a logical consequence in the modern university; activism. Indeed, the Woke ethos considers activism to be a legitimate and essential role for an academic.

There is no shortage of examples of such "opposition to oppression" and academic activism nowadays, be it through Antifa or Black Lives Matter protests, the de-platforming of people with viewpoints incongruous with CSJ, or the canceling of university professors for using words deemed to be beyond the pale. From within the academy, and within the professoriat, this ethos builds upon a transition from the importance of the Marxian means of economic production, to the Neo-marxian means of cultural or epistemic production; from the shop floor to the Ivory Tower. It is also closely tied to Dutschke's notion of the "long march through the institutions."

The opposition of oppression in universities actually serves two purposes. The first is to rid universities of antiquated worldviews developed by oppressor European males to perpetuate their own privilege. The second is to replace these with those adhering to the CSJ perspective.

Accordingly, and given the degree to which universities are permeated with oppression (each person, each program, each class, each administrative process), there are an infinite number of "sites" of oppression from which to oppose. As a result, just about every interaction, every function must be challenged, problematized and opposed. It is for this reason that the Woke professoriat will attempt to oppose, thwart and coerce into the CSJ mold everything over which they can have influence. This means every course syllabus, every course program and every administrative procedure.

Given the importance of controlling the means of cultural and epistemic production, the biggest prize, and the events that often lead to the most outright conflict, is the hiring of a professor. All means will be used to ensure that a Woke professor is hired, and that a non-Woke scholar is not. Such opposition has been moving steadily upwards into the hierarchy and bureaucracy of academia from departments, to faculties, to university administrations, to journals, disciplinary associations, government funding agencies and government departments.

1.4 Oppression is a Continuum

Section 1.3 above described the Critical Social Justice (CSJ) belief that oppression is everywhere. That it is everywhere, however, is not to say that all oppression is equal. Oppression can be looked at disaggregately or aggregately. Looking at oppression disaggregately involves considering the amount of oppression in a given act.

The amount of oppression in a given act can be seen on a continuum. The disaggregate continuum of oppression can be seen as a range of acts roughly from relatively minor insults (such as microaggressions) to wage discrimination to torture to violence, sexual violence and murder/genocide. While individual acts of oppression may be seen as indicative of larger and more encompassing forms of oppression, the oppression of individual acts can, ultimately, be ranked.

Of course, people don't experience only one single act of oppression, they are typically seen to experience (many) different acts of oppression. As a result, oppression is more characteristically seen as aggregate. The total amount of aggregate oppression can also be seen on a continuum. The amount of oppression affecting different groups can be summarized according to many different characteristics of group identity such as sex, skin color, gender, sexual orientation, hearing ability, etc.

As such, women suffer a given amount of oppression, black people suffer another amount of oppression. In addition to this, identities (and therefore oppression) can be overlapping. As a result, a black woman suffers the oppression of being a woman and she also suffers the oppression of being black. On top of that, a black woman suffers the oppression of being a black woman. This is a special kind of oppression over and above the oppression suffered as a result of just being black and just being a woman. It is said thus that to understand and evaluate oppression, one needs to consider the "intersection" of identities (and oppression) for any individual (Crenshaw; 1990).

8

Identities can be combined into a "matrix of oppression." Matrices of oppression can be used to understand and evaluate the oppression any given individual suffers according to their overlapping group membership. Naturally, there are some groups of people who don't experience oppression, but experience the opposite: privilege.

White people, males and heterosexuals are considered not to experience oppression, but rather privilege. As such, oppression can be seen on a continuum with the most oppressed being people at the intersection of many different oppressed group identities (e.g. indigenous, female, lesbian). At the other extreme are those with intersections of privilege, such as white heterosexual males. Every individual can be found along the continuum of oppression. Figure 1.1 presents a schematic of this continuum. The identities and location on the continuum of oppression shown here are indicative and not necessarily definitive.

Figure 1.1: Stylized schematic of the continuum of privilege and oppression.

1.5 The Woke Political Project

The Woke worldview and ethos has gelled around the following political project; the retributive redistribution of resources according to group identity known as "equity." The redistribution is intended to flow from "oppressor" groups to historically "oppressed" groups.

The "equity" project is not typically presented in this light. It is more commonly presented as "just" the redistribution of resources according to group identity to "redress" historical imbalances. It is thereby justified by suggesting that the goal will be achieved once imbalances are redressed. Imbalances themselves can be reckoned upon any number of criteria be they professorships, research funding, citations, etc.

This implies for example that professorships along every dimension in which they can be classified (university, faculty, department, discipline, etc.) should be allocated to different identity groups according to their representation in a given target population. The target is often undefined but when it is defined it can be national, state or university-level population. In practice this implies that 51% of professorships in every department should be women, 13% (in the US) should be black, etc. Similarly, 51% of citations should be of women scholars, 13% of black scholars, etc. Any deviation from such targets along any dimension is considered to be indicative of bigotry according to the identity group being considered (sexist if considering females, racist if considering blacks, etc.).

Increasingly, however, the goal of redressing historical imbalances is making way towards retribution. There is ample evidence for this throughout academia in North America as universities and governments seek no longer to meet targets, but rather exceed them. For example, Le High University's strategic plan for diversity, equity and inclusion seeks to "Meet or exceed national diversity demographics for the group of faculty hires in the next five-year period."[1] Similarly Canada's Carleton University has the objective to "Continuously meet and exceed all equity hiring targets"[2] for its positions for federally funded research chairs.

1.6   A Woke-related Typology of Participants

Universities consist of students, faculty, staff and administrators. To varying extents, they all play a role in the decisions that affect the administration of the university. Faculty play the most important role and have the most influence since they are around for so long and are found at many levels of the hierarchy of the university, including most administrative positions. I refer to members of university communities who can influence university

---

[1] https://engineering.lehigh.edu/about/dei/strategic-plan
[2] https://carleton.ca/coris/wp-content/uploads/Carleton-CRC-Equity-Diversity-and-Inclusion-Action-Plan-December-17-20....pdf

decisions, policy and governance as "participants." With respect to the influence of the Woke perspective, participants can be classified according to six categories: the Woke, the Woke-adjacent, opportunists, dissidents, latent dissidents and the uninitiated.

1.6.1   The Woke

The Woke are people who are conscious of the Critical Social Justice perspective and who adhere to it. That they adhere to it is to say also that they agree with it. As such, this is a three-dimensional definition with the dimensions being: knowledge/consciousness of, adherence to, and agreement with the CSJ perspective.

For the most part, the Woke come from the fine arts, the humanities or the social sciences, where they have been introduced to, trained in and radicalized by the Critical Social Justice perspective. There remain some pockets of the social sciences that have not been completely subsumed by the CSJ perspective (e.g. economics, some quantitative sub-disciplines of psychology & political science and philosophy) and so some participants in these disciplines are not Woke.

1.6.2   The Woke-proximate

The Woke proximate are people not trained in, or familiar with, Critical Social Justice theory. Some are completely unaware of it, while others may know that it exists but not know very much more than that. While the Woke proximate are not knowledgeable about CSJ, they do adhere to, and agree with, the perspective, or at least with its prescriptions. The Woke proximate will agree broadly, for example, with "diversity, equity and inclusion" initiatives such as affirmative action and reparations. They will also typically agree with (and believe in) doctrines such as systemic racism, and support Woke advances. Politically, they will be on the (extreme) left, be collectivist and interventionist in outlook and often anti-capitalist. The Woke proximate tend to come from the natural sciences or other quantitative disciplines, especially those with environmental vocations, such as environmental science, climate science, etc.

There are three reasons why professors from these disciplines are likely to be Woke proximate. First, for the most part they are well-intentioned. They support "social justice" and don't see or understand the difference between traditional social justice and Critical Social Justice. They believe that what is advocated by Critical Social Justice is the virtuous evolution of social justice developed by those (scholars) who have focused their attention on it.

Second, especially for professors with an environmental vocation, the environmental and CSJ perspectives dovetail on a number of issues, particularly with respect to the perceived moral turpitude of liberal, western, capitalist society. This commonality is rarely theoretically motivated since the Woke proximate don't really have a theoretical canon comparable to CSJ, given their natural science-dominated training. To the extent that it is theoretically motivated, it is likely to be influenced by various shades of "red & green" Marxism (see e.g. Bahro (1984); Bookchin (1982)) or "scientific" environmental catastrophism (e.g. Carson (2002)).

Third, the Woke proximate, like Woke professors themselves, are typically "action-oriented." That is, they believe themselves to have an important moral and activist vocation. The result is that while they are often trained in scientific, or quantitative, positivistic fields, they are disconcerted by the fact that science is amoral. Given the strength of their own (environmental) convictions, they can be persuaded that strict scientific rigor, or logical and argumentative coherence can be softened if a cause is sufficiently important and urgent.

It is important to be aware of the Woke proximate. First, it is common to believe that people trained in the sciences will be less susceptible to the attractions of the Critical Social Justice perspective. The truth, however, is that they can just as easily adhere to and agree with it, despite not being very knowledgeable about it. As such, they can hold the balance of power in situations and thereby enable CSJ advances. This is important to recognize when understanding how to manage the dynamics of situations, and as we'll see later (See Section 3.), how to repel Woke advances.

Given their tendency to agree with the CSJ perspective, support CSJ advances, and their "scientific" appearance, the Woke proximate are also the unwitting vanguard of CSJ in the STEM fields. They represent thereby the greatest threat to fields not yet dominated by the CSJ perspective. Also, given their scientific background, although I haven't seen this done successfully, I think they can be made to recognize the threat to science that the CSJ perspective represents, and so potentially become Woke dissidents (see Pincourt (2021a) for an essay that tries to do just that).

1.6.3 Opportunists

Opportunists are participants who may or may not be aware of the Critical Social Justice perspective and who may or may not agree with it. They do, however, adhere to it and will advocate for it, or at least not challenge it. These participants appear to think that the CSJ perspective will dominate in the future and don't want to be disadvantaged by not going along with it. Opportunists are found in all disciplines but are most likely found in business disciplines, engineering and other STEM fields. They are less common in the fine arts, social sciences and humanities mainly because the vast majority of participants in these disciplines are Woke. For the most part, opportunists cannot be counted on to help counter CSJ, apart, possibly in the context of secret ballot voting (see Section 3.9).

1.6.4 Woke Dissidents

Dissidents are those who know (or are conscious of) the CSJ perspective but do not adhere to it, are critical of it and who actively work against it. Since few from STEM fields know very much about the CSJ perspective, dissidents come primarily from the fine arts, humanities and social sciences. They are very much in the minority in these disciplines and can come from across the political spectrum. There are more and more dissidents emerging from business and STEM fields, however, as CSJ is making inroads there.

I use the word dissident because of a characteristic of the CSJ perspective itself, and our culture that is increasingly swayed by its norms and rules; that people are not allowed to question or disagree with it. The current canceling, de-platforming and quashing of dissent from the CSJ perspective parallels accounts of the quashing of counter-revolutionary ideology in the Soviet bloc as described by, among others, Aleksandr Solzhenitsyn. Solzhenitsyn was associated with people in the former Soviet Union who criticized and worked against Soviet ideology, referred to collectively as dissidents.

1.6.5 Latent Dissidents

Latent dissidents may or may not know about the Critical Social Justice perspective. If they do know of it, they'll only know it superficially. Most importantly, however, they will likely instinctively disagree with the CSJ perspective, recognizing it as illogical and inherently contradictory. They'll likely also find it's prescriptions to be deleterious to the search for knowledge and to science in general. Latent dissidents are most often found in STEM fields and business schools. They also represent the greatest hope for resisting the complete dominance of the Critical Social Justice perspective in universities; especially if they can be converted to outright dissidents.

1.6.6 The Uninitiated

I'll occasionally refer to the category, the "uninitiated." This is not a mutually exclusive category. It includes all those that are not familiar with the CSJ perspective and who don't agree with it. They may or may not adhere to it, but they don't know anything about it. It includes both opportunists and latent dissidents, although not the woke-proximate.

Chapter 2

Wokecraft

The first part of the manual seeks to familiarize readers with the Critical Social Justice perspective and the Woke themselves. This part transitions to describing the strategies and tactics used by the Woke to advance the CSJ perspective in universities; what I call "wokecraft." The term wokecraft is meant to evoke covert strategies and techniques used in other specialized fields like spycraft in espionage. The analysis (of key concepts, principles, strategies and tactics) is based on my experience as a professor in a North American university for more than a decade. The analysis itself builds on concepts and terms discussed in the previous chapter. There is a bit of conceptual background that is necessary to understand wokecraft, so I'll start with that.

2.1 Key Concepts of Wokecraft

There are a number of concepts that help to define and explain the contours of wokecraft. The concepts themselves are both conceptual and definitional.

2.1.1 Situations

The wokecraft I describe is that undertaken by Woke participants at events in which the participants have decision-making abilities. Using rhetorical convention (Lundberg and Keith; 2008), I call such events "situations." Situations include departmental assemblies, departmental academic committees, hiring committees and all other committees and bodies in the university with representation from the various participants and where they can formally impact decisions (departments, faculties, senates, boards of governors, etc.).

2.1.2 Sites of Oppression

Section 1.3 explains how the Woke ethos insists that oppression is everywhere and needs to be opposed wherever it is found/believed to exist. Oppression is seen to manifest itself at "sites" of oppression. Sites can be physical locations, but the notion is much broader than that. Oppression can be contained in course curricula, an application form, or in the content of a website. Any such "place" where oppression can be seen to exist, and therefore opposed, is a "site" of oppression.

2.1.3 Problematization

While oppression is assumed to be always present, due to the postmodern political principle, however, it is often believed hidden in plain sight. Problematizing[1] is the mechanism by which oppression is identified, or "exposed." It involves providing an explanation of how a particular person, situation or circumstance is oppressive, or embodies, perpetuates or legitimizes oppression in one form or another, particularly when this is not immediately apparent.

Problematization can range from the very small to the very grand. At the small end of things is the identification of microaggressions. Microaggressions are acts that people perform typically without even being conscious of

---

[1]https://newdiscourses.com/tftw-problematize/

them that marginalize, exclude, oppress or insult. If a white person were to ask, for example, where someone who appears to be of Asian descent comes from, this could be problematized and considered a microaggression. The reason for this is that by recognizing this difference, the person asking the question is implicitly assuming that the other person does not come from "here," which is exclusionary. On a grander scale, it might be said that while common people in Western societies see themselves as free and prosperous, the reality is that they are oppressed by the capitalist economic system without their even being conscious of it. In this example the whole of Western society is "problematized."

2.1.4   Goals, Advances and Incursions

"Goal" is shorthand for CSJ goal. Goals are found on a continuum from short- to long-term. Short-term goals are prosaic and focused, but are typically aimed towards the achievement of longer-term goals. A short-term goal may be as simple as including the word "critical" in a course outline. Long-term goals are more ambitious and less focused. An example of a long-term goal is the overthrow of structures of oppression inherent in a university. An advance is an attempt to reach a CSJ goal. A successful advance (e.g. the inclusion of the word "critical" in the final course outline) is referred to as an incursion.

2.1.5   Entrenchment of the CSJ Perspective

The degree to which the CSJ perspective is entrenched varies from situation to situation and can be thought of as a continuum. At one extreme are situations at which the CSJ perspective is completely absent. This could be a department where no one has ever heard of the CSJ perspective, and where its notions have not been introduced explicitly or implicitly. Such departments are increasingly rare, but to the extent that they exist, they are most likely to be found in engineering, commerce and the most theoretical scientific departments. If members of such departments are conscious of the CSJ perspective, it will be referred to as "political." It is also likely to be considered harmless, even if it is seen as a bit strange.

At the other extreme are departments where all professors are adherents and advocates of the CSJ perspective or simply, Woke. This is the case in the vast majority of the social sciences (except, perhaps economics) humanities, fine arts and most reliably in "studies" departments such as women's studies, queer studies, etc.

The CSJ perspective will be entrenched to different degrees in different situations depending upon the composition of the participants present. The degree to which it is entrenched will be a function of the proportion of Woke participants, and the history of CSJ incursions. The more Woke participants there are, and the more incursions there have been, the more entrenched the CSJ perspective will be. Given the zeal of the proponents of the perspective and the inexorable tendency of the perspective to increase its influence, it is helpful to define stages of entrenchment of the perspective that can be used to describe any situation (a department, a faculty meeting, university council, etc.).

A situation with no Woke participants, where CSJ notions have not been introduced and no advances have been made is unentrenched. Early-stage entrenchment is characterized by a small number of Woke participants whose status as Woke may or may not be known, a few subtle and non-forceful advances have been tried and incursions have been made. Late-stage entrenchment is characterized by a significant proportion of Woke participants and several incursions have succeeded. Full entrenchment is characterized by a majority of Woke participants, more radical advances with no attempt to hide them, and the silence of participants not adhering to the perspective.

2.2 Principles of Wokecraft

The entrenchment of the CSJ perspective is in large part because of the successful adoption of a few principles engaged in by Woke participants. They are as follows.

2.2.1   Always Try

Ultimately, every Woke attempt at opposition to oppression can be seen as an attempt to entrench or further entrench the CSJ perspective within the university or, an "advance." A key aspect of the Woke ethos is an obligation to oppose and resist oppression, while not opposing is tantamount to complicity with oppression. As a result, in every situation where oppression is identified, Woke participants will try to make an advance. This amounts to always, under all circumstances, trying to push the envelope.

2.2.2   Least Amount of Force Necessary

While advances will be attempted in all situations where oppression is identified, it's worth noting that wokecraft is practiced with different degrees of forcefulness under different circumstances. As a general approach, the least amount of force necessary (LAFN) will be used to advance the Woke agenda in any situation. This implies only using as much force as is necessary to make a successful advance.

While the forcefulness of techniques used is mitigated by the LAFN principle, the forcefulness of techniques is intensified according to three considerations: the importance of the issue, the amount of resistance encountered, the proportion of Woke members in a given situation, and how entrenched the CSJ perspective already is.

The greater the perceived importance of a particular example of oppression in any given instance, the more forceful will be the techniques used. The importance of a particular act or site of oppression is related to how much oppression is perceived (see Section 1.4) to be associated with the act or site. The more oppression, the more forceful will be the techniques used.

The forcefulness of techniques used will increase with the amount of resistance encountered. If little resistance is encountered, there is little need to apply forceful techniques, as is consistent with the LAFN principle. As the amount of resistance increases (people ask questions or disagree) more forceful techniques are used. Should people strongly oppose and try to prevent the advance, even more forceful techniques will be used.

The forcefulness of techniques is directly related to the proportion of Woke participants. There is a group effect so that the higher the proportion of Woke participants, the more likely is the use of more forceful techniques. In some cases, more forceful techniques simply become possible with more Woke participants. In other cases, a higher proportion of Woke participants can lead to a faster escalation in the forcefulness of techniques used.

Finally, the forcefulness of approaches increases as the CSJ perspective becomes more entrenched. In early-stage entrenchment advances will be subtle. As the CSJ perspective becomes more entrenched, advances will be more forceful. This is because as the perspective becomes more entrenched, there will typically be more CSJ adherents and less resistance. Moreover, the ability to roll back incursions once they have been made is more difficult, and as a result it is less important to temper any advances.

2.2.3 Try to Go Unnoticed until It's Too Late

The LAFN approach is adopted because it is (consciously or unconsciously) recognized that greater forcefulness will draw attention to any advance, when the aim is to camouflage advances as much as possible. The aim is for advances to be covert and unnoticed until they are firmly entrenched. It is for this reason that it can be difficult to detect advances during early-stage entrenchment, and difficult to reverse them once they come to light.

2.2.4 Every Advance Should Succeed

In making advances, the Woke are faced with a dilemma. While sites of oppression are everywhere and advances must always be attempted, it is also necessary to go unnoticed as long as possible. This tension is resolved by making sure every advance succeeds. As a result, advances need to be understood in the short and long terms. The long term goal is to overthrow structures of oppression inherent in universities. At the same time, it is recognized that this long term goal must be advanced, and not threatened by, short term advances. This principle has an important influence on the strategies used to make advances. Early-stage advances will emphasize short term, small advances chosen to make significant advances in the long term.

2.2.5   The Ends Justify the Means

Two aspects of the Critical Social Justice (CSJ) perspective together have a dramatic influence on Woke rules of engagement: Woke epistemology, and Woke zealotry. Woke epistemology is based on the notions that all knowledge and knowledge systems are socially constructed by oppressor groups, and constructed in such a way to advantage oppressor groups to the detriment of the oppressed. This implies that not only is what we consider knowledge oppressive, but the methods by which we obtain any knowledge are also inherently oppressive. This implies, for example, that the scientific method is oppressive, as are methods for the establishment of knowledge such as evidence, argument and even logic.

The second important aspect influencing Woke rules of engagement is Woke zealotry. This zealotry was discussed in the Woke ethos section (see Section 1.3). Essentially, the Woke believe in the CSJ perspective with a fervor that is difficult to appreciate outside of religious movements. They believe the perspective to be uniquely true and just. Moreover, they believe they have a responsibility to propagate it and counter oppressive worldviews and particularly the modern, liberal understanding of the world that has developed since at least the Enlightenment.

These two aspects together remove from the Woke ethos any need to subscribe to traditional rules of engagement when deemed necessary. As a result, given the moral fervor as well as the belief that traditional rules of engagement are in and of themselves oppressive, such rules can be abandoned at any moment.

Techniques abandoning traditional rules of engagement are more forceful, and in keeping with the LAFN principle, will typically only be used when more forceful methods are deemed to be required. An important thing to recognize and be prepared for, however, is that the traditional rules of engagement and fair play will and are abandoned, often with a viciousness that is truly terrifying and with little notice. The ends are believed to justify the means.

2.3   Key Tools of Wokecraft

The principles of wokecraft are implemented using a number of tactics and strategies. At the base of many tactics are two very common tools.

2.3.1   The Woke Dog Whistle

For the past few years I've been puzzled by a couple of things related to Critical Social Justice. The first is how it has been advancing and infiltrating inexorably into every crevice and instance of my work (as a university professor) and social milieu. The second is that the people around me who are not Woke don't notice it, or don't notice it until it has already happened or is too late. There is more than one reason for this, but one of the most important is the Woke dog whistle.

Dog whistles (Galton's whistle) are whistles that emit sounds above the sonic range that humans can hear. They're used to call or train dogs without disturbing the humans that train them or those nearby. The term has also been adopted in political discourse to refer to the use of coded language to garner support from target groups while avoiding opposition from non-target groups. A lot of words used by the Woke are in fact dog whistle terms.

Such dog whistle terms work, and are so insidious for two reasons. The first is that the terms used allow the Woke to communicate to each other. In particular, it allows Woke individuals to recognize each other as Woke - it is essentially a verbal group identifier. The second reason is that Woke dog whistle terms have traditionally been (perhaps intentionally) harmless sounding words, especially to the uninitiated. The two together make them textbook dog whistle terms.

The classic example of Woke dog whistle terms is the term "critical" itself. This word has been particularly useful in academia since it goes completely unnoticed by the uninitiated, and is in fact a word that is universally looked upon favorably in academia. "Critical" for the Woke refers to the CSJ perspective. "Critical" to the uninitiated is considered to be the raison d'être of the university, as in "teaching students to think critically." As a result, a critical agenda can be advanced and implemented, in plain sight, but with only the Woke (and dissidents) being conscious of it.

2.3.2 Woke Crossover Words

In the previous section I started trying to explain an enigma. How could the CSJ perspective be so successful at spreading, while the uninitiated often don't even notice its spread, and when they do, it's often too late? I also described how this is done with Woke dog whistles. Woke crossover words are related to Woke dog whistles. Woke dog whistles are used as dog whistles because they are seemingly harmless and can hide in plain sight. They seem harmless because their Woke meaning is camouflaged by the use of crossover words. Crossover words have multiple meanings. One meaning is its commonplace definition (like you might find in a dictionary). The other meaning is the Woke definition. Crossover words have three characteristics.

First, the words are common and non-technical sounding. They are rarely words outside of the grasp and use of most people who interact with the Woke. In the last section I discussed the word "critical," but words like "racism," "equity," "diversity," and "intersection" are typical crossover words used in common parlance. Less common and more technical words like (random example) "hermeneutics" are rarely redefined.

Second, their usual (commonplace) definitions are well-understood and believed to be commonly accepted. The uninitiated, when they hear "critical," "diversity" or "intersection" have pretty clear definitions in their minds of these words, and they won't be concerned about their meaning because their definitions are typically thought to be clear; to themselves and to everyone else. The Woke definitions of these words are, however, *very* and *radically* different. Crossover words are non-technical intentionally so that it is not necessary to have discussions about their definition.

Third, crossover words often (although not always) sound "nice." If there are two words that describe the same concept, the nicer sounding word will be used. That is why we often see "inclusion," but not normally "exclusion" used as a crossover word. This is useful because it makes it difficult to question their meaning. This is what makes the combination of crossover words and the Reverse Motte & Bailey Trojan Horse tactic (see Section 2.4.3) particularly effective.

2.4   Woke Micro-tactics

The principles of wokecraft and its key tools are combined in a series of micro and grand tactics. The main micro-tactics are as follows.

2.4.1   Subverting Liberal Decision-making

There are a number of Woke micro-tactics that take advantage of and subvert traditional liberal good-faith group decision-making. Before looking at these micro-tactics, it's necessary to consider what traditional liberal decision-making involves.

Liberal, Good-faith Debate and Decision-making

Section 2.2 on the principles of wokecraft outlined the general principles that are the basis for tactics adopted by Woke participants advancing the Critical Social Justice (CSJ) perspective in universities. In that section I also described how for Woke participants, the ends justify the means. By this I meant that traditional liberal rules and norms of engagement in discussion, argumentation and decision-making are considered to be optional and secondary to the goal of advancing the CSJ agenda. That claim requires a definition of what traditional liberal rules and norms of engagement are.

It's important to note that I'm not using the term "liberal" here in the modern North American political sense, i.e. of the contemporary progressive left. Rather, I'm referring to the liberal tradition stemming primarily from the Enlightenment and the English/Scottish Enlightenment in particular. Pluckrose and Lindsay (2020) and Levin (2013) provide overviews of the liberal tradition in this sense.

In this tradition, norms and in some cases explicit rules (e.g. "Robert's Rules"), have developed to guide fair discussion, argumentation, debate and decision-making. According to this tradition, all parties participating in a situation are encouraged to respectfully and honestly express their opinions on the topic of interest. They are also expected to consider others' opinions respectfully, charitably and in good faith. This means that one tries to understand the spirit of what someone intends to say. At the same time, the respectful (and possibly forceful) expression of disagreement is expected and encouraged should it be felt.

Importantly, disagreement is seen as fundamental to good debate and decision-making. Disagreement is particularly important since while people can generally convince themselves of their own opinions, it is more difficult to convince others. Others are likely to bring up things that a proponent has not considered thus forcing them to robustly argue their positions. This counters the well-recognized tendency that we have towards confirmation bias (finding evidence that supports our own positions, see e.g. Haidt (2012)).

Finally, liberal decision-making emphasizes argumentation, logic and the presentation and evaluation of evidence in support of opinions that are expressed. In this tradition, there is a tacit tendency towards consensus in decision-making. While consensus is by no means the goal, and despite the importance of disagreement, in normal circumstances, people will try to adjust discussions and decisions to conform to a tacit consensus position. When consensus is not possible, mechanisms such as voting can be used to arrive at decisions, if not necessarily to the resolution of disagreement.

These norms and rules have served us well and have brought us the extraordinary and prosperous societies that make up the US and Canada today. Tactics subverting traditional liberal decision-making take advantage of these norms and rules by using the opportunities the tradition provides to advance CSJ, while not according them to those not adhering to the CSJ perspective. They are particularly important because the subversion of these norms allows Woke participants to have more influence and "punch above their weight," and this is indeed, why they are used. What follows is a series of explicit tactics used in this subversion.

Woke Insistence on the Informal

Typical and traditional liberal decision-making is characterized by formalized methods to propose topics of discussion, rules by which they are discussed, and how decisions about them are made (see e.g. Robert's Rules of Order). At the least, this involves the use of agendas (agreed-upon beforehand), times for the beginning and ending of meetings and discussion items, as well as methods by which decisions will be made, such as voting. These rules have evolved over time for many reasons, some of which are that they help to ensure that each person has the right to their own opinion and to influence decisions based on their own opinions, without necessarily having to divulge them. This last point is in fact, the foundation of modern democracy.

Woke participants will insist on informality in meetings. Arriving on time is not considered important, adhering to pre-determined items on the agenda or pre-determined times for discussion are not important either, particularly if there is another issue they would prefer to cover. "Flexibility" is emphasized so that meetings can develop "organically." Attempts to insist on adhering to agendas or rules will be belittled for being unnecessarily formal or "bureaucratic."

From the CSJ perspective, insistence on the informal is justified primarily by maintaining that traditional liberal rules governing decision-making have been developed and used to perpetuate structures of power favoring oppressors to the detriment of the oppressed. As such, these rules are considered "instrumentalist." In this vein, it may be maintained that no rules are necessary, or that different forms of equally-effective and legitimate decision-making methods (e.g. healing circles) originating from oppressed identities and cultures, and which are thereby non-oppressive, can and should be used instead. It may also be maintained that such rules are simply indicative of whiteness and are thereby inherently racist. As such, not adhering to traditional rules amounts to resistance against oppression and indeed with the decolonization of the university. Often, it is simply intimated that such rules are not "cool," a surprisingly effective technique.

Should a given situation, however, not go in the direction of supporting a CSJ advance, Woke participants will appeal to formal rules to defend against a retreat. In such situations they may insist that not enough discussion was allowed, or on some other technicality. While this is not consistent with resistance against liberal decision-making, it is consistent with its subversion and with the wokecraft principle that the "ends justify the means." The insistence on informality allows Woke participants to have more power in the decision-making process and that is why it is advocated.

Enmity towards Secret Ballot Voting

A specific micro-tactic by which informality is used to subvert decision-making is by preventing secret ballot voting, which will be strenuously resisted (unless, Woke participants are in the majority). That Woke participants prevent decisions being made by secret ballot is extremely important in explaining their oversized influence. Doing so makes it easier to bully, hector, shame and threaten people to support Critical Social Justice advances, or at least, not resist them. Instead, there will be (as described in Section 2.4.2 below) an attempt to have decisions made by "consensus." This is because coercing consensus is an effective Woke bullying tactic. In addition to the standard justifications for eschewing traditional forms of decision-making described above, the following justifications may be made to discredit and prevent secret ballot voting.

First, it can be criticized for being "divisive" while consensus will be lionized for being inclusive. Second, it can be criticized for being too "binary." According to CSJ, being binary (having only two alternatives or categories) is problematic because categorization itself is considered to be a form of oppression.

Running down The Clock

Another advantage (and reason for an insistence on informality) is the flexibility it provides for delaying discussion, or running down the clock. The clock can be run down by filibustering or by forcing additional topics onto an agenda. It can be done with two goals.

The first is simply to prevent an item from being discussed at all at a meeting. This might be undertaken if there is to be a policy or decision advocated that would work against CSJ goals. The second is to increase pressure when a particular CSJ goal is being advocated, or to ensure big decisions are made without sufficient time to question or challenge them. In this context, discussions will be continued so that a meeting will go over time and anyone not supportive of a CSJ advance will surrender their resistance in exasperation and/or because they have other commitments. This is very effective when secret ballot voting is prevented. In that context it increases a time-related pressure, but prevents an easy resolution through secret ballot voting, thereby increasing the likelihood that CSJ advance will succeed.

Recruiting Woke Allies

Section 2.1 on the key concepts of wokecraft described the different stages of entrenchment of the CSJ perspective. Ultimately, there is a clear correlation between the degree of entrenchment and the proportion of Woke participants. A higher proportion of Woke participants leads to the ability to use more forceful techniques and ultimately to make advances more easily and of greater impact. It is for this reason that attempts will be made at all stages to increase the number of Woke allies.

Ideally, the addition of Woke allies will be done at the expense of Woke dissidents or the uninitiated. Such additions or replacements will often be advocated for, or justified on the basis of "diversity" and "inclusion." The most important context of recruitment is in the hiring of tenure-track faculty. Almost unlimited resources will be devoted to this since it is, ultimately, the most important vector for the entrenchment of the Critical Social Justice perspective in a university.

Emphasizing Emotion and Experience

This micro-tactic involves presenting an argument related to how a Woke participant feels in order to support a CSJ advance or goal, or argue against an initiative counter to CSJ goals. This is a rhetorical technique that will typically involve the Woke participant positioning themselves within an identity or intersection of identities and therefore of oppression, and then expressing how the given item of discussion makes them feel from this position.

The micro-tactic is intended to elicit emotion, sympathy and perhaps guilt in the audience and thereby to influence their opinion with respect to a given initiative. This tactic is justified by at least two reasons from the CSJ perspective.

First, since according to the CSJ perspective all knowledge is socially constructed, inherently oppressive, and an inaccurate representation of reality, experience is seen as the only way (accurate) knowledge of reality can be obtained. Second, since argumentation, logic and the presentation of empirical evidence are considered to help perpetuate and reproduce systems of oppression, it is legitimate to ignore them and concentrate on experience and emotion. Advancing experience and emotion as evidence in a liberal context is considered anecdotal and myopic, and of limited value in group decision-making.

Demand Charity but Don't Extend It

Two key aspects of traditional liberal decision-making are good faith in discussion and argumentation, and charity in interpretation. Arguing in good faith entails an attitude where participants discuss and argue with the aim of establishing the truth or the best outcome for a given situation or decision. The Woke ethos, being myopic and zealous, aims solely to advance social justice goals in the university. As such, the Woke stance involves the abandonment of good faith in discussions.

Charity on the other hand involves making an effort to understand what people are trying to argue while providing people the benefit of the doubt if they do so imperfectly. A common Woke technique is to abandon any pretense of charity of interpretation, which often is done by problematizing what people say independent of what they intended to say.

This is justified from the CSJ perspective because it is assumed that people unconsciously speak to and perpetuate the oppressive power structures to which they are subject. As such, even what they may have "meant" to say is meaningless in contrast to the uncovering of the oppressive meaning that they cannot help but express. This was first referred to as the "death of the author" by Roland Barthes (1968).

While charity is not extended to interlocutors, Woke participants will insist on it for themselves and their own arguments. If their arguments are interpreted in a negative light, or if unflattering implications of their arguments or logic are evoked, they will maintain that their argument was not treated charitably. They may claim that they "just" meant some other uncontroversial or innocuous point. They may also go on the offensive maintaining that the unflattering interpretation or evocation is a function of a position of privilege, of wanting to perpetuate existing structures of power or of being racist or bigoted.

2.4.2   Woke Bullying Tactics

This subsection concentrates on micro-tactics that rely on bullying and intimidation to limit opposition to, and disagreement with, CSJ advances and goals. It also builds on the section describing liberal debate and decision-making (Section 2.4.1).

Tactics using bullying and intimidation are among the most forceful micro-tactics. As such, they tend to be reserved for situations where the Woke perspective is well entrenched, there is a high-proportion of Woke professors, the act or site of oppression is particularly important or a combination of all three of these. The section begins with tactics undertaken by individuals and then to those done in groups, and as such progress from less to more forceful methods.

Making Things Awkward

In a situation, and during discussions, an important Woke tactic is to make things awkward. Situations are rendered awkward by Woke participants hectoring, insisting too much upon something and "not letting things go." Woke professors will commonly insist on their perspective to a point that it makes everyone uncomfortable. The intention is that the non-Woke participants, to avoid awkwardness, will give in to Woke demands or at least give up any resistance to them. This tactic exploits the liberal expectation to be respectful of others' opinions, as well as the tacit general tendency to find a consensus. In a sense, this tactic tries to force a consensus around a position that is possibly held by only one person. As such, it is a form of bullying.

Ad hominem Attacks

Ad hominem attacks involve criticizing the person making an argument rather than criticizing the argument itself. Should someone, for example, question a CSJ notion like the omnipresence of oppression, a Woke participant might accuse the speaker of being complicit with oppression, not caring about oppression, endeavoring to preserve their own privilege, etc. This tactic simply side-steps liberal decision-making norms by focusing on the individual in an attempt to make them feel bad or discredit them. This is also used as a threat. The threat communicates first of all that the Woke participant is willing to use personal attacks to get their way. Second, the threat communicates to anyone else who dares to challenge a CSJ notion that they too could be subject to the same treatment.

Assume Guilt, Expect Proof of Innocence

In the previous section I evoked a particular *ad hominem* attack; that of accusing a speaker of complicity with oppression. This *ad hominem* attack is worth highlighting since it is so common and often effective. The reason it is particularly effective is that it reverses the traditional liberal principle (see Section 2.4.1) of the presumption of innocence until proven guilty. It is effective because people typically feel as though they need to defend themselves against an accusation, regardless of whether the accusation has any merit. This is destabilizing and can cause someone to retreat from a position.

Intentional Misinterpretation

This involves a Woke participant intentionally misinterpreting what some-one opposing a CSJ advance or goal has said. It is typically combined with problematizing what the person has said. The misinterpretation of what was said will normally be intended to reflect badly upon the non-Woke speaker.

An example would be a discussion related to a policy of identity-based hir-ing at a university. A non-Woke professor might voice concern about such a policy by describing it as discriminatory towards identities not the target of the policy, and contrary to a dedication to universal rights. A Woke profes-sor could intentionally misinterpret what was said and interpret it as mean-ing that the non-Woke professor didn't care about racism. They might fur-ther problematize it by saying that the concern was voiced from a position of privilege and represented an (unconscious) attempt to perpetuate that privilege. This tactic has the same aims as the *ad hominem* attack. That is, to discredit anyone opposing a CSJ advance or goal, to make them feel bad and/or guilty, as well as to serve a threat not to oppose Woke goals and advances.

It is contrary to liberal norms of good-faith and charity of interpretation. It can, however, be justified in the CSJ perspective for two reasons. First, the Woke ethos (Section 1.3) compels the Woke to always seek out and expose oppression that they believe to be omnipresent. As a result, such a misin-terpretation could be depicted as uncovering hidden oppression. Second, it can be justified by appealing to the CSJ subject principle, which insists that people "speak into" the oppressive structures into which they are embed-ded and which they perpetuate, even without their knowing. This is what Roland Barthes referred to as the "death of the author" Barthes (1968).

Using Consensus as Coercion

Advocates of the CSJ perspective emphasize the importance of consensus in decision-making. Consensus is considered important because it is related to an avowed guiding principle of the perspective (as well as crossover word), "inclusion." The idea is that consensus in decision-making leads to better decisions because it includes "all" perspectives. The implication of the use of "all" perspectives is that traditional, liberal methods only include the perspective of oppressors. As such, the goal of all discussions, debates and decisions is to arrive at consensus. As a result, there is a strong pressure not to disagree and to conform to emerging consensus opinions and decisions.

Voicing disagreement (with a CSJ advance) will be looked down upon and will typically be considered "divisive." Divisive means that a person is blocking, or working against consensus, the Woke goal of decision-making. The result of this pressure to conform is ultimately bullying and renders consensus decision-making little more than coercion. The goal of consensus cannot easily be enforced by one person, so this is a tactic requiring multiple people and is a "team effort."

This tactic is clearly in opposition to liberal decision-making norms as it discourages disagreement and tries to coerce consensus. In the liberal tradition, while consensus is considered nice to have, it is not in and of itself a goal. Methods that seek to coerce agreement and discourage dissent are anathema to good decision-making in the liberal tradition.

Piling on

This is one of the most forceful and intimidating micro-tactics. It involves a number of Woke participants challenging one individual. It will typically involve an individual expressing views that question, are not supportive of, or are not consistent with a CSJ advance in a given situation.

A combination of legitimate argumentation will be used with any number of other tactics (*ad hominem* attacks, intentional misinterpretation, using appeals to consensus as coercion, etc.), typically one after the other in what amounts to a barrage of attacks. The subject of such a pile-on may very well not even be able to respond between individual volleys from Woke participants. Piling on is reserved for situations in which the CSJ perspective is almost fully entrenched.

Piling on, while intimidating, may or may not be consistent with liberal decision-making. The degree to which it is consistent is a function of the tactics used by the individual Woke participants. If legitimate argumentation is used, and if the subject is allowed to respond between volleys, this could amount to the regular cut-and-thrust of robust debate. Sadly, this is rarely how a pile-on takes place.

Canceling and De-platforming

The most forceful Woke bullying tactic is also the one that is the best known: canceling and de-platforming. Canceling and de-platforming involve coordinated personal attacks, typically through online sources, and social media in particular.

They are normally launched on account of a participant holding unpopular public opinions. They can also result from a participant resisting Critical Social Justice advances in the context of their duties (e.g. a departmental meeting). Such attacks commonly lead to demands at all levels of a university to prevent the accused from teaching, rescind academic rank, and even fire altogether. The attacks can be initiated by professors, but more commonly come from other participants and particularly students. This phenomenon is not restricted to academia. What is extraordinary, however, is that such attacks can be successful in universities and can involve the firing of tenured professors for their opinions or for behaving consistently with their conscience. The aim of canceling and de-platforming is clearly to suppress resistance to Woke advances and goals.

This is perhaps the most iconic illiberal, Woke tactic. In the liberal tradition, ideas are to be allowed into the marketplace of ideas where they can be subjected to rational, public criticism. This was indeed the most important liberal innovation. Preventing people from expressing their opinions on pain of losing their livelihoods is the most extreme illiberal tactic in modern democratic societies.

2.4.3   The Reverse Motte & Bailey Trojan Horse

Whereas previous sections described numerous Woke micro-tactics, this section concentrates on only one micro-tactic, what I call the "Reverse Motte & Bailey Trojan Horse." I concentrate only on this tactic in this section since it requires relatively elaborate explanation, and because I think it is perhaps the most effective of the Woke tactics in universities. To understand the Reverse Motte & Bailey it is necessary to understand the Motte & Bailey[2] technique as well as the Trojan Horse analogy.

The Motte & Bailey Rhetorical Technique

The first description of the Motte & Bailey technique was by Shackel (2005). The terms motte & bailey refer to a form of medieval European castle introduced into England by the Normans. The motte is a well reinforced tower on a mound that is easy to defend, but unpleasant to stay in. The bailey is the courtyard below the motte surrounded by a protected ditch and palisade that is less secure and more difficult to defend, but more pleasant to inhabit.

The Motte & Bailey strategy involves a proponent who wants to advocate a difficult-to-defend, extreme position (the bailey). When (or if) the extreme position is challenged, the proponent retreats to an easily defendable and easily acceptable position (the motte). The key to the strategy is a hidden false equivalency of the extreme and easily acceptable positions.

An example of how this might play out in a university setting is the following. A Woke professor might advocate for a lower proportion of white professors on a hiring committee based on the (extreme) CSJ claim that white people are inherently, unconsciously and irredeemably racist. This is the bailey position, the extreme position "where" the CSJ advocate would like to be. Should anyone question such claims, by for example asking for evidence of inherent, unconscious and irredeemable racism in white people, the advocate would retreat to an uncontroversial "motte" position. The advocate might, for example, respond "What, so you don't believe that racism exists?" This move is intended to destabilize the person questioning the claim, who likely wouldn't want to claim that racism doesn't exist. To the extent that the strategy works (which it often does), it is based on the false equivalency between the (uncontroversial) claim that racism exists and the

---

[2]https://podcasts.apple.com/us/podcast/stealing-motte-critical-social-justice-principle-charity/ id1499880546?i=1000473920836

(extreme) claim that all white people are racist.

A Trojan Horse

A Trojan Horse is a strategy of subterfuge involving a covert insertion of forces behind enemy lines followed by a surprise attack by the inserted forces. The term originates from Virgil's popularization of events around the Trojan war. After a ten-year long unsuccessful siege of Troy, the Greeks built a huge wooden horse in which a team of elite soldiers hid. The Greeks pretended to sail away, leaving the horse. The Trojans then brought the horse into the walls of Troy as a trophy. The following night, the hidden soldiers opened the gates of the city for the Greek army, which had sailed back under cover of night.

The Reverse Motte & Bailey Trojan Horse

The Reverse Motte & Bailey Trojan Horse strategy involves three elements. First, unlike the Motte & Bailey, a motte (uncontroversial) position is proposed by one or multiple Woke participants. Second, the motte position is usually inserted through the use of a Woke crossover word. Third, once the Woke crossover word has been accepted and integrated into the situation (this can take a long time), it is then maintained by the Woke participant(s) that the correct interpretation of the crossover word is the extreme Critical Social Justice meaning. As such, the Trojan horse is the Woke crossover word, which goes unnoticed until the overt advance is made.

A classic situation embodying the Reverse Motte & Bailey Trojan Horse is the negotiation around the description of a new departmental hire. Consider for example a position proposed in Public Infrastructure Finance. Perhaps the original intention of the proposed hire was to find an expert on how public infrastructure can be paid for, to fill a lack of expertise in the field in the department. The title would be accompanied by a description of expertise and research areas sought, such as:

"The department is seeking a candidate with an expertise in public infrastructure finance in areas such as, but not limited to: electrical, sewerage, stormwater, transportation, communication infrastructure, in developed or developing world contexts."

A Reverse Motte & Bailey Trojan Horse in this context would begin with a Woke professor suggesting the inclusion of a crossover word or concept into the description. In this example, a Woke professor might suggest the addition of the clause "...including research at the intersection of these areas." Uninitiated professors are not likely to understand why it would be necessary to include such a clause, but they likely wouldn't want to make a fuss about something that appeared so harmless. This is the introduction of the motte position through the word "intersection."

The term intersection here serves as a Trojan Horse for the CSJ meaning of intersection (i.e. of intersectionality). The bailey position will be introduced, and the Trojan Horse uncovered later on.

A typical way by which the bailey position will be introduced is in the selection of candidates after the job has been announced and applications have been submitted. At this stage, the Woke professor(s) will maintain that the word "intersection" refers to its radical, extreme, CSJ definition. Based on this, they will argue that Critical Social Justice candidates should be considered in selecting candidates to be interviewed, even though the original nature of the position was clearly not intended to be a CSJ position. This thereby increases the probability that a CSJ professor will be hired, one of the most important victories for the Critical Social Justice perspective in universities.

2.4.4 Telegraph, Project and Subvert/Invert

The expression Telegraph, Project and Subvert is inspired by James Lindsay's notion of the "Iron Law of Woke Projection." As the expression suggests, it involves three components: telegraphing, projecting, and subverting/inverting.

The telegraphing component imbues a proposal, action, reaction or concept with a malevolent Woke interpretation. This malevolent interpretation is then projected as being the true (although perhaps unconscious) motivation or intention of the advocates, and the proposal merely a tactic to advance the true intention. As such, the first two components amount to an accusation of an illegitimate, "problematic"[3] justification for a proposal inserted using a deceitful tactic. The third component involves a subversion where the Woke participant uses the problematization of the adversary's position to delegitimize the adversary and their proposal.

It is easy to see how this could be an effective tactic. People are for the most part sensitive to being, or being seen as, hypocritical, even if they are not. To have one's intentions and integrity (even if they are "only" unconscious) questioned and problematized can be highly destabilizing; perhaps destabilizing enough to back down from advocating a position or proposal.

A variation of this tactic is to replace the subversion step with an inversion. This involves actually advocating for what is being criticized, but using a different label for it, to Woke ends. The latter is often used in combination with crossover words and their Woke opposites.

An example of straightforward telegraphing, projecting and subverting might be a debate around a proposal to use secret ballot votes in decision making in a department. (See sections 2.4.1 and 3.7 for more discussion on secret ballot voting.) Proponents of secret ballot voting may advocate for its use on grounds that it allows people in more precarious positions to participate in decision making without having to publicly express their opinions about it. In doing so, they may provide as an example the situation of untenured professors.

Someone telegraphing, projecting and subverting the proposal could do the following. They might claim that the proposal (especially because of highlighting the example of untenured professors) could be seen as a way to threaten untenured professors so that they don't express their opinions (telegraphing). They may then imply that that was (perhaps unconsciously) the intention of the proponents (projecting). Finally, they could use these to advocate against the proposal (subversion).

An example of telegraphing, projecting and *inverting* is a typical skirmish

---

[3]See 2.1.3.

relating to a proposed policy of preferential hiring for people of color. A non-woke professor may oppose such a hiring practice on the grounds that it is racist (because it involves distributing resources on the basis of race). In such a context, a Woke participant may then say that making this claim could be seen as an attempt to perpetuate current structures of oppression and thereby legitimizing racism (telegraphing). Moreover they may very well say that the claim is being made from a position of privilege and that perhaps unknowingly it was made with that aim in mind (projecting). Finally, the Woke participant may further claim that in this context, supporting the policy actually challenges the existing structures of oppression and as a result is in fact not racist, but anti-racist (inversion).

In this example we see how the Woke participant is able to do a number of things. First, they attempt to delegitimize the original argument against racist hiring practices. Second, they invert the argument by advocating for something that they accuse their opponent of having advocated, that is legitimizing racism. Third, this is all facilitated by using the crossover word racism and its Woke opposite, anti-racism.

2.4.5   Other Woke Micro-tactics

This section includes a grab bag of other Woke micro-tactics included for completeness, even though they are not thematically coherent.

Moral Hubris and High Ground

This tactic is primarily rhetorical. Woke participants will support advances with unwavering confidence, hubris and priggishness. At the same time, it will be claimed or intimated that any challenge to a Woke advance is morally bankrupt and unimaginable. Staking out the moral high ground confidently serves primarily to repress any dissent. It can be very intimidating and a successful technique.

Always Support a Woke Ally

In any given situation, Woke professors will support Woke allies making an advance. This is pretty much independent of the Woke advance in question. The provision of meaningful or additional arguments is not really necessary, although arguments will be presented. Arguments used may be logical, although they can also be specious, disingenuous and often simply shameless. What is important is to demonstrate support while attempting to repress dissent. The number of Woke allies (consistent with the Least Amount of Force Necessary principle) providing support will increase as a function of the perceived amount of dissent and difficulty in ensuring a successful advance.

Obfuscation with Technical Jargon

This technique is used in many different contexts, but will commonly be found when supporting a Woke ally. Arguments will be advanced using all manner of Critical Social Justice jargon, whether it is appropriate or not. Since there is so much CSJ jargon and since it often sounds serious and authoritative (e.g. epistemic oppression, discursive aggression, heteronormativity, etc.), and since few non-Woke participants know what they mean, it can be used with impunity to support an ally. The goal of the use of such jargon is typically to intimidate and suppress any dissent.

DEI as Cover for Recruiting Woke Participants

The terms diversity, equity, inclusion among many other positive-sounding Woke words (see Section 2.3.2 below) are used as cover for recruiting woke participants. The concepts are useful for the CSJ perspective because they seem at first glance unambiguously positive. Also, questioning them is easily painted as bigoted or racist. It is for these reasons that diversity, equity and inclusion will be used to advance many different initiatives, particularly for recruiting new members to a given situation or site of oppression (committee, department, discipline, etc.).

In reality, the terms are used to recruit people that agree with, can be convinced of, or can be forced to comply with, the CSJ perspective. Only very rarely (I've actually never seen it, but I assume it has happened thanks to unusually principled Woke participants) will participants be recruited based on diversity, equity or inclusion but not actively support, or at least not resist, the CSJ perspective.

Dramatic Departure

Dramatic departure is a two-stage tactic. In the first stage, it involves a Woke participant dramatically and conspicuously threatening to leave a situation in protest of a decision going against a Woke advance. It may be accompanied with an appeal to the Woke advocate's identity and/or to an explicit or implicit accusation of bigotry on the part of those opposing the advance.

An example of this would be a Woke participant saying something like "...as an x-identity person, I feel that this decision erases my identity." The threat to leave is used to elicit sympathy for, as well as induce guilt associated with, the Woke participant and their position. Other participants may be influenced in their decision and consider abandoning their resistance to a Woke advance.

If the threat is not successful, the Woke participant may follow through with the threat and depart (the meeting, the committee and in extreme cases, a department or even university). This is ultimately a last-ditch, Hail Mary type tactic. Its effects can be positive or negative.

The departure of the Woke participant can ultimately be beneficial since there will be one fewer Woke participant in the situation. Unfortunately, the tactic can also have long-lasting effects. It can introduce a miasma of doubt within the situation and may cause longer term damage as the initial intention of the threat (to elicit sympathy and guilt) may work in the longer term. In this way it is a bit like a land-mine planted that may or may not go off. Whether the effects are negative or positive will have to do with the resilience of the situation or institution.

Passive-Aggressive Opposition

In early stage entrenchment, Woke participants policies seen to work against a CSJ agenda, through passive-aggressive behavior.[4] Passive-aggressive behavior is characterized not so much by explicit opposition, but rather by a combination of overt non-opposition but covert opposition. A typical example would be a participant not agreeing with a policy but agreeing to help with its implementation. During the implementation phase, however, they will not do what they were supposed to do, not adhere to deadlines or do it erroneously to slow progress of the proposal. This can cause initiatives to completely lose momentum and not be implemented at all. This is done mostly in early stage entrenchment because it is discreet.

2.5 Summary of Woke Micro-tactics: Subterfuge, Exaggerating Support & Quelling Dissent

Until now, I've concentrated on the Woke worldview, the Woke themselves, the Woke ethos, general Woke concepts, principles and the specific tactics used to advance the goals of the Critical Social Justice perspective in universities. In this section I categorize Woke micro-tactics building on concepts from previous sections. The categorization helps to summarize micro-tactics, but will also serve as a framework for understanding wokecraft and how to protect against it.

On a whole, Woke micro-tactics can be placed into three categories: subterfuge, exaggerating support, and quelling dissent. While tactics in each of the categories can be used in almost all situations, there is a correlation between the category of tactics used and the stage of entrenchment of the Critical Social Justice perspective. Similarly there is a correlation between the stage of entrenchment and the forcefulness of the micro-tactics.

---

[4]https://www.webmd.com/mental-health/passive-aggressive-behavior-overview

It's useful to recall the different stages of entrenchment (see Section 2.1). In early-stage entrenchment, there is a small proportion of Woke participants. Advances are subtle and characterized by the least amount of force. Mid-stage entrenchment involves a higher proportion of Woke participants, although less than the majority. Advances at this stage are less subtle and more forceful than in early-stage entrenchment. Finally, in late-stage entrenchment, there is a high proportion of Woke participants (perhaps the majority) and advances and tactics are the most forceful.

Tactics of subterfuge in early-stage entrenchment are used to help establish the presence of the CSJ perspective. That is, CSJ notions are introduced and planted, non-woke initiatives are thwarted through passive-aggressive behavior, allies are identified and the ranks of the Woke swelled, if this can be done subtly.

Mid- and late-stage entrenchment are aimed directly at altering the perceived balance of power and acceptance of the CSJ perspective. Mid-stage entrenchment involves actively and overtly recruiting Woke allies, and appeals to exaggerating the perceived numbers of Woke participants. This leads to the impression that there is more support than there actually is.

Late-stage entrenchment on the other hand concentrates on quelling dissent, which necessarily requires the use of more forceful tactics. The combination of the latter two categories of micro-tactics is intended to give the impression that the CSJ perspective is more accepted than it is. This impression allows the Woke to "punch above their weight." This thereby facilitates Woke advances and further entrenches the perspective. Figure 2.1 represents the relationship between CSJ entrenchment, tactical categories and the forcefulness of advances and tactics.

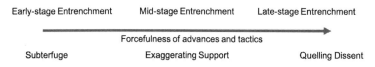

Figure 2.1: Relationship between CSJ entrenchment and forcefulness of tactics.

Using this schema, we can place Woke micro-tactics into the three tactical categories. Subterfuge is associated with early-stage entrenchment and tactics involving the least amount of force. Subterfuge involves the use of tactics that are difficult to spot and that use emotional manipulation. As such, the tactics qualifying as subterfuge include the use of Woke crossover words, Woke dog whistles, emphasizing emotion and experience, most tactics subverting liberal decision-making, passive-aggressive opposition, and the motte of the Reverse Motte & Bailey Trojan Horse.

Exaggeration of support is associated with mid-stage entrenchment and the tactics used are more forceful. Tactics used to exaggerate support include actively recruiting Woke allies, staking out the moral high ground, the bailey of the Reverse Motte & Bailey Trojan Horse, supporting Woke allies, using technical jargon in support of Woke allies and dramatic departure.

Finally, the quelling of dissent is done primarily through forceful bullying and thereby includes tactics such as *ad hominem* attacks, using consensus as coercion, piling on, canceling, de-platforming and firing.

2.6 The Grand Tactic - Woke Viral Infection

The previous section considered many individual micro-tactics that are used to make Woke advances in universities. These micro-tactics can be seen as being in the service of the larger scale "grand" tactic, Woke Viral Infection, inspired by Lindsay 2020b.

As described in Chapter 3, the Woke political project is equity (the retributive redistribution of resources according to group identity), with redistribution flowing from historical "oppressor" groups to historically "oppressed" groups. The achievement of equity is to be done by overthrowing all existing institutions (committees, departments, faculties, universities, disciplines, funding agencies and governments), each of which is considered a site where oppression needs to be exposed and overturned.

In practice, such overthrow is ultimately done by gradually replacing non-woke with Woke participants. Since professors are the foot soldiers of university bureaucracies, the knowledge production system, and disciplinary machinery, the overthrow of the entire academic system is done through the recruitment of Woke professors. The advance is done first through departments, and from departments, to the rest of universities, disciplines, funding agencies and governments. When possible, this involves the removal of non-woke professors (see e.g. Section 2.4.2), but given the constraints posed by tenure, the key approach is to overwhelm rather than to purge. While most successful until now in the fine arts, social sciences and humanities, attempts to overthrow STEM fields are well underway.

The overthrow is undertaken in much the same way as a virus infects a cell. The allegory of the virus has been used both by proponents of the Critical Social Justice perspective (e.g. Fahs and Karger (2016)) as well as its detractors (e.g. Lindsay (2020a)). Viruses attach and then infect cells thanks to receptors on host cells. Receptors recognize and attach to proteins useful to host cells, but viruses can mimic the proteins and thereby attach to host cells. Once a virus is attached to a cell, it can enter it and use the cell's own machinery to replicate itself. Once replicated, copies of the virus can break free from the host cell to infect others and continue its spread (Freudenrich and Kiger; 2020).

Continuing with the analogy of the virus, we can think of sites of oppression as being the equivalent of cells that can be infected by the CSJ perspective. Each site of oppression has different receptors with the most common receptors being the "critical" and "diversity" receptors. These receptors can and are used to infect sites/cells with the CSJ virus. The most common and important sites for the spread of the CSJ virus are university departments and disciplinary entities since they are the gateways into the machinery and apparatus of the entire knowledge production system. Traditionally, infection has taken place primarily thanks to the "critical" receptor. More recently infection has taken place through the "diversity" receptor. Finally, the most worrisome current battlefront is infection through the "social/society" receptor in STEM fields.

2.6.1   Critical Receptor Infection

The CSJ virus infects via the critical receptor in the following way. First, it takes advantage of an openness of academics to a general spirit of scepticism by appealing to the word "critical." The word critical itself is a crossover word that doesn't mean critical in the sense of critical thinking, but rather holds the *radical* Critical Social Justice meaning (see Section 2.3.2 on crossover words). Second, it is said that the current site of oppression is deficient because of a lack of a critical perspective. Third, the identification of this weakness goes hand-in-hand with a proposal to incorporate the critical perspective, most commonly by including additional Woke participants. As such, the tactic can be described as: introduce the notion of criticality, denounce the site as not being sufficiently critical, incorporate new critical participants.

In a typical departmental context, this three-step process would result in a proposal for hiring a professor that adopts a "critical" stance on whatever the department happens to concentrate on, e.g. *critical* legal studies, *critical* literary analysis, *critical* geographies, *critical* race, etc. Once this advance is made, the critical "scholars" will use Woke micro-tactics to recruit other critical scholars until the department is overwhelmed and the CSJ perspective is fully entrenched. The virus is also spread as students trained in the department leave to infect other aspects of the university and disciplinary bureaucracy. It is through this process that most departments and disciplines in the fine arts, social sciences and humanities have come to be dominated by the CSJ perspective.

2.6.2   Diversity Receptor Infection

Increasingly, infection with the CSJ perspective is coming through the diversity receptor. The CSJ virus infects via the diversity receptor in the following way. As with the word critical, the word diversity is a positive-sounding crossover word with a radical meaning, synonymous with equity. First, the nice sounding merits of diversity are trumpeted. Second, the site in question is criticized for being deficient because of insufficient diversity. Third, proposals to increase diversity are advocated. Infection through the diversity receptor is a little more subtle (see Section 2.4.5). That is, the goal of a recruitment based on diversity is less diversity and more the recruitment of participants that either adopt, will not resist, or who can be made to comply with, the Critical Social Justice perspective. In other words the recruitment of a Woke participant is made using diversity as a cover.

In a typical disciplinary context, such as a scholarly society of some form or another, the process might look like this. First, the merits of diversity to the discipline will be emphasized. Second, the discipline will be criticized for its lack of diversity along any number of dimensions such as sex, skin color, sexual orientation, etc. Third, policies to increase diversity will go hand-in-hand with attempts to recruit new participants bringing a new diverse (and "critical") perspective to the discipline. Such recruitment typically involves the recruitment of Woke or woke-proximate participants, which is in fact, the central purpose of increasing of diversity.

2.6.3 Social Receptor Infection in STEM

Finally, it is also through this process that STEM fields are being infected, albeit slightly more subtly. It is more subtle because it is not yet possible to advocate in favor of *critical* engineering or *critical* physics.[5] In these fields, the critical perspective is more commonly introduced through sociological expressions such as "social" or "society."

As with "critical" and "diversity" these words seem harmless, positive and unambiguously beneficial. It is for this reason that one sees attempts to hire professors, or start new departments or sub-disciplines related to sociological or societal aspects of a STEM discipline, such as computing *and society* or engineering *and society*. Such participants, sub-disciplines, institutes or departments are gateways for the Critical Social Justice perspective in STEM fields. Once participants enter through these gateways, they work to discredit and delegitimize STEM fields by insisting on the need for "critical" or more "diverse" perspectives in these fields. Once this is done, these disciplines as well are put in the service of reproducing the CSJ perspective in departments, faculties, universities and beyond.

---

[5]Although this is coming. See for example (Gutiérrez; 2017).

Chapter 3

Counter Wokecraft

The second chapter of this manual concentrated on the various concepts, strategies and tactics making up wokecraft. This part introduces and describes how wokecraft can be countered in your department, faculty, university or beyond.

3.1 How to Spot Wokecraft before It's Too Late

The first task, before being able to counter wokecraft, is to know how to spot it. There are a number of strategies that should be used towards this end.

3.1.1 Take It Seriously

Many participants, while conscious of some of the most egregious results of the Critical Social Justice perspective, do not take it seriously, and don't think it can affect them. This is most common among professors in disciplines and departments in which the CSJ perspective is not entrenched. It can be observed most often in engineering, and sciences without an environmental vocation. For the most part, these professors know nothing of the CSJ perspective, and are thus uninitiated. They might sardonically associate Woke unrest with disciplines exhibiting little *gravitas* such as those in the fine arts, humanities and most of the social sciences. They might also consider the unrest to border on the comical and be thankful that their disciplines are not affected.

It is not, however, only the uninitiated who fail to take the CSJ perspective seriously. Woke dissidents can be dismissive, scornful and contemptuous of CSJ. Since they know something about the perspective, they can lull themselves into believing that the absurdity and obvious contradictions of the perspective mean that serious people can't possibly succumb to it. As a result, they can conclude that it represents little threat to them or their discipline. This, of course, has now been proven at best na'ive and at worst simply false.

The truth is that the number of disciplines where the CSJ perspective is not entrenched and where there is little threat of entrenchment is decreasing rapidly. It is now clear that STEM fields are the new front line in the Critical Social Justice struggle (see e.g. Abbot (2017); Domingos (2021); Kay (2020)) towards the domination of universities. Also, the situation in any discipline, department, university, etc. can change very quickly, often with (seemingly) no warning, and often with no way to turn back. As a result, the CSJ perspective and its ability to expand into any and all disciplines must not be underestimated. Professors in all disciplines need to be on the lookout for signs of the advance of this movement, and importantly, take it very seriously.

3.1.2 Be as Familiar with the CSJ Perspective as Possible

The better you understand the CSJ perspective, the more effective you can be at spotting it, and countering its advances. This is not to say that you shouldn't attempt to counter it unless you have read every last article in the journal "Gender, Place & Culture." While the CSJ literature is vast and for the most part inaccessible to uninitiated readers, this does not mean you can't understand the basics. This is partly due to the fact that increasingly there are sources that can be understood by non-specialists. The best single source to understand the Critical Social Justice perspective available now is Pluckrose & Lindsay's Cynical Theories. Allan Bloom (2012) and Stephen Hicks (2011) provide excellent descriptions of the long historical roots and development of the perspective. The "New Discourses" website[1] is also excellent and includes an "encyclopedia" of CSJ terminology.[2]

It's also partly because the perspective and its related phenomena can be surprisingly effectively reduced to, and understood by, three principles. The three principles are the knowledge principle, the political principle and the subject principles (see Section 1.2). If you know these principles, just about any CSJ term, sub-discipline, phenomenon and tactic can be understood. As a result, a little time devoted to understanding the perspective can be surprisingly fruitful. This can help you to understand, spot, explain to others, and counter CSJ advances.

3.1.3   Be Vigilant

As discussed before, dissident professors need to be aware that the Woke ethos exhorts adherents to always try to make advances for CSJ goals. They also need to be aware that always trying to make an advance is a key principle of wokecraft (see Section 2.2.1). As a result, it is necessary for dissidents to continually be on the lookout for signs of Woke advances. In mid- to late-entrenchment, this is not difficult since Woke advances will be obvious and vocal. Before entrenchment, however, or in early-stage entrenchment, advances will tend to be subtle. It is for this reason that it is particularly important to be vigilant before entrenchment or during early-entrenchment; the CSJ perspective can gather momentum quickly. Once it has momentum, it can be very difficult to stop.

---

[1] https://newdiscourses.com/
[2] https://newdiscourses.com/translations-from-the-wokish/

3.1.4 Watch for Woke Words

The best way to be vigilant is to watch for Woke words. There are two types of words to watch for: Woke crossover and overt Woke words and expressions. As described in Section 2.3.2, Woke crossover words are simple words with commonplace, well-understood meanings, but which also have radical CSJ meanings. Crossover words are used as dog whistles so that Woke participants can identify and signal to each other. Woke participants identify allies to find common cause and to unite so they can exaggerate support for Woke advances. Crossover words are also used to covertly inject CSJ concepts into all aspects of administrative and intellectual infrastructure; from course outlines to webpages to professor job descriptions for recruitment, to institution-wide policies, etc.

At critical moments, the Woke meaning of previously injected crossover words will be insisted upon to advance CSJ goals. This is known as the Reverse Motte & Bailey Trojan Horse tactic (see Section 2.4.3). The list of crossover words is not as long as that of overt Woke words, but it is important to be aware of them; partly because of how they are used covertly, and partly because of what a successful tactic the injection of Woke concepts is by using them.

Here is a list of the most common Woke crossover words:

- critical
- decolonization
- discourse
- diversity
- embed
- empowerment
- equity
- inclusion
- intersection
- justice
- liberation
- knowledge(s)
- narrative
- perspective(s)

- privilege
- race/racism
- resistance

If you see or hear any of these words, especially if someone tries to insist on them (e.g. add them to a document, course description, website, etc.), recognize that this is likely a Woke advance.

Overt Woke words and expressions are easier to spot, but are less likely to be used before entrenchment, or in early-stage entrenchment. It's worth being aware of them all the same, since they can appear before or in early-stage entrenchment. They're easy to spot because they stand out. Below is a list of categories of overt Woke words. The best source to find such words is the New Discourses Social Justice Encyclopedia.[3]

1. **Words that appear highly technical and that often originate in philosophy:** Typical words in this category are words like dialectic, epistemology, hegemony.

2. **Words that appear to combine multiple words that are not normally associated:** They often appear unintuitive as well. Typical words and expressions in this category are binary privilege, colorstruck, compulsory heterosexuality, epistemic exploitation, cultural competence, meta-narrative, etc.

3. **Words that appear to have been made up:** This category includes words like autosexuality, colorism, deadname, episteme, cisgender, heteronormativity, minoritize.

4. **Words that are spelled differently than they normally are:** These often use strange letters, particularly "x." Examples of these words are latinx, mathematx, womon, wimmin, xdisciplinary.

5. **Words that describe Western society, but which are used in a decidedly negative sense:** Common words in this category are the West, liberalism, capitalism, modern, modernity.

---

[3]https://newdiscourses.com/translations-from-the-wokish/

6. **Words traditionally with a positive association in common language, but which are used negatively or derogatorily, particularly those relating to the Western philosophical tradition:** Examples of these are logic, reason, argument, Enlightenment, freedom, free will, choice, individuality, etc.

7. **Words and expressions that explicitly contain references to group identity, while also seeming invented:** This includes words like blackness, whiteness, white privilege, white adjacency, fat shaming, ableism, gender traitor.

8. **Words and expressions that sound decidedly bad or evil:** They are often antonyms to positive-sounding crossover words (e.g. exclusion vs. inclusion). Common words like this are: colonialism, conflict, oppression, bias, false consciousness, struggle.

9. **Words that are opposites of crossover words:** Crossover words often have complimentary Woke opposite words to which they are juxtaposed. So, for example racism is often juxtaposed with anti-racism, colonization with decolonization, exclusion with inclusion, segregation with desegregation, etc.

If you hear any of these words or expressions, it is an indicator that the person using them, or advocating their use, adheres to the CSJ perspective. You should also expect that its use is part of a Woke advance. If you hear any words that you've never heard before, but could fall into these categories, you should look them up in the Social Justice Encyclopedia.[4]

3.2   General Counter Wokecraft

The previous section concentrated on how to spot Woke advances and wokecraft. This is the first on counter wokecraft. It concentrates on general approaches.

---

[4]https://newdiscourses.com/translations-from-the-wokish/

3.2.1 If You See Something, Say Something

One of the reasons the Critical Social Justice (CSJ) has progressed so effectively through our society is that even when people recognize an advance, they will often not say anything. This is partly because advances so often seem so small and so unobtrusive that saying something about them seems not worth the trouble. The trouble, of course, is feeling uncomfortable and the sense of not getting along with your colleagues, being "divisive" and not being a team player. It's important to recognize that these feelings are all consequences of Woke strategies and tactics.

I've previously discussed how it is a key principle of wokecraft to always try to make an advance. Always trying to make advances, even when inappropriate, is intended to take advantage of people's good will and generally non-confrontational natures. Making advances when they are inappropriate also makes things awkward causing people to be uncomfortable, encouraging them to let the advance pass, and discouraging them from opposing it. Appeals to "consensus" and using consensus as coercion (see Section 2.4.2) are also tactics that will be used to force people to "go along to get along" and make people unwilling to oppose Woke advances.

At the same time, dissidents who don't say anything, don't recognize two things. First, they don't appreciate the long term impacts of not saying something. Small advances can (and are intended to) become big advances in the future. Second, people don't appreciate how effective simple and even mild opposition can be - particularly in early-stage entrenchment. I am increasingly told of CSJ advances being disarmed simply by having raised a principled but mild objection.

Of course, the consequences of saying something are not always just mild discomfort. As the CSJ perspective becomes more entrenched, more extreme bullying tactics (*ad hominem* attacks, pile-ons and attempts at canceling) are more likely to be used, and they can be much more threatening. Opposition in this context is certainly not for the faint of heart. It is for this reason that saying something before, or in early-entrenchment is worthwhile. It will represent mild discomfort for long term protection against wokecraft.

Saying something when you see something helps to counter all three of the main types of Woke tactics. It will counter subterfuge by exposing advances as soon as they are perceived. Second, it will reduce the ability of Woke participants to exaggerate support for a given advance. Third, by expressing opposition it flies in the face of attempts to quell dissent. In addition, it will also help other potential dissidents recognize you as an ally.

3.2.2   Remain Suspicious and Sceptical

Given the traditional liberal principle of good faith and charity of interpretation, it is natural to give the benefit of the doubt to a Woke participant when they are making an advance. Woke advances often involve the presentation of both motte and bailey positions at the same time (see Section 2.4.3 on the Motte & Bailey rhetorical tactic). This has two results. The first is that the Woke respondent can appeal to the Motte & Bailey tactic. This involves retreating to an uncontroversial motte position if an (extreme) bailey position being advocated is challenged. The second, however, is that a well-intentioned interlocutor may provide the Woke participant the benefit of the doubt by thinking to themselves that while they may not agree with the bailey position, the motte position is reasonable. Finally, they might think to themselves that the Woke participant advanced the bailey position (perhaps out of passion of belief), but was really "just" trying to advance the motte position.

This might play out in the following way. Imagine a situation during a departmental meeting with at least one Woke participant and a well-intentioned non-woke participant. A Woke participant might start with an uncontroversial motte claim (for which there is a great deal of evidence) about a performance gap between black and non-black applicants to a graduate program, and that this is a probable cause for the relatively low representation of blacks in the program. The Woke participant may then continue with an extreme bailey position that the performance gap is caused by the systematically racist nature of society, and that any performance gap has more to do with racist indicators that are used to evaluate performance (such as GREs) than any actual performance differences. Finally, the Woke participant may therefore advocate for the removal of GREs as a way to evaluate applicants to the graduate program on this basis.

The well-intentioned non-woke participant would likely be sympathetic to the concern that the Woke participant has presented (the motte position). At the same time, they may not agree with the bailey claim about systemic racism and the GREs being inherently racist. As such, they may be tempted to give their colleague the benefit of the doubt, perhaps by saying to themselves that their Woke colleague doesn't really believe the claim they're making about systemic racism.

In situations such as these, it is very important to take Woke participants at their word and remain attuned to this type of argumentation. Most importantly, one needs to remain suspicious and sceptical of such arguments, the people making them and critically not extend them the benefit of the doubt. (This is also a good situation to steal the motte and bomb the bailey - see Section 3.2.5 below.)

3.2.3 Always Have an Alternative to Propose

Since the Woke will always try to make an advance (see Section 2.2.1), it's necessary to thwart an advance whenever one is observed. Thwarting an advance involves both opposing it, but also having an alternative to propose instead. If a Woke participant tries to recruit a Woke ally to a committee, oppose the attempted recruitment and propose a dissident ally. If a Woke participant proposes a new CSJ hire, oppose it and propose a non-Woke alternative.

3.2.4 Never Let Them Add Their Words

Very often, Woke advances are as simple as the addition of a few words. The most effective and insidious related tactic is the Reverse Motte & Bailey Trojan Horse (see Section 2.4.3). Before, I explained that it is important to say something if you see something. But what exactly are you supposed to say? In this context you should say that the extra words are not necessary and should not be included. This has two advantages. First, it is likely that the words will not be included because you did say something. Second, it will likely force the Woke participant to identify themselves as such. This is advantageous in order for you to properly recognize Woke colleagues, but as importantly, it will do this for other non-Woke colleagues as well.

In order to be successful in this endeavor, you'll need to be able to recognize Woke words and especially Woke crossover words (see Section 3.1). You'll also need to have a clear idea of your position on the issue in question, and in particularly that a CSJ interpretation of the issue cannot be allowed. If someone wants to add the word "critical" to a newly proposed course outline on data analysis, you might respond: "this is intended to be a course on technical aspects of data analysis and is not intended to be a course adopting a critical perspective. That perspective is available in other courses in the department." It probably won't come to this, but it might be useful to be familiar with what the "critical" perspective implies and in particular its three core principles (see Section 1.2).

3.2.5   Stealing the Motte and Bombing the Bailey

Another approach that can be used to "say something if you see something" is "Stealing the Motte and Bombing the Bailey".[5] As described in Section 2.4.3 the Motte & Bailey rhetorical strategy involves advancing a radical and difficult-to-defend position but then retreating to an easily defended position if the radical position is challenged. Stealing the motte while bombing the bailey involves recognizing the legitimacy of the motte position, but directly challenging the bailey position.

In the section on the Motte & Bailey above (see Section 2.4.3), the example of a Woke professor advocating for a lower proportion of white professors on a hiring committee was evoked. It was explained that such a proposal might be justified based on the extreme (bailey) CSJ claim that white people are inherently, unconsciously and irredeemably racist. A typical Motte position could be retreated to if challenged, by asking whether the challenger didn't believe that racism existed.

---

[5]https://newdiscourses.com/2020/05/stealing-motte-critical-social-justice-principle-charity/

Stealing the motte in this context would involve responding by saying that obviously racism exists. Bombing the bailey on the other hand involves strenuously denying the bailey. One might say for example that claiming that all white people are inherently and irredeemably racist is itself racist, that there is no evidence for such a claim, and that the argument itself relies on a fallacious (CSJ) understanding not only of reality, but of what constitutes racism.

This approach is a similar to, but a more assertive and generalizable approach than "never letting them use their words." It has the same advantages but can be more authoritative and convincing. Being able to use it effective requires a stronger mastery of the Critical Social Justice perspective but should be used if possible.

3.2.6   Co-opting Woke Advances

It is sometimes possible to co-opt a Woke advance for counter wokecraft, although this should be done cautiously. It amounts to using a Woke advance to introduce ideas or themes that fly in the face of the CSJ perspective. I've heard of an example of this where Woke faculty proposed to "decolonize" a curriculum they judged to be too Eurocentric. A dissident co-opted the situation by agreeing to change the curriculum in exchange for including units on Marxist Utopian experiments in the Soviet Union, China and Southeast Asia.

Such co-opting can be successful if it can subvert Woke messaging or advances, but it does not come without its risks. The most important is a risk of unintended consequences. For example, in the short term the dissident curriculum may actually be taught, but the precedent of using Woke language and concepts as a justification to mold curriculum can easily be used in the future to greater Woke advances.

3.2.7   Go as High up The Chain as You Can

Another consideration in countering wokecraft is where precisely you should counter it. As suggested from above, you should try to counter it whenever you come across it. The reality is though that the higher in an administration you can practice counter wokecraft, the more influence it will have. This means that if you have opportunities to have influence at higher levels, you should take them. For example, it's better to be on a faculty curriculum committee than a departmental curriculum committee, and it's better to be on a university senate than a faculty council. If you can influence donors, all the better, if you can influence your state government, better still.

While everyone is overwhelmed with their current duties and reluctant to take on more, this does not necessarily mean more work. In any case, academics are expected to contribute to university administration. As such, when negotiating your duties, you should privilege those duties that allow you to have influence at the highest level possible.

3.2.8   Make Sure to Vote!

As a participant at a university, you are often asked to vote for different positions within the university hierarchy. These can be positions for deans, associate deans, union boards, governing boards, etc. These positions are important for the direction that universities take and usually are decided based on only a few votes.

There are two consequences of this. First, it is easy for Woke, Woke-proximate or opportunist participants (see Section 1.6) to get elected to these positions. This is a problem in and of itself, but becomes more important as more Woke participants are represented on the committees for which they are running. The more woke participants, the more the Woke perspective will be entrenched (see Section 2.1.5), the more forceful the Woke will be and the more radical will be the advances they will try and likely succeed with. Second, since such positions play on so few votes, these are probably the most "efficient" votes you will have in your life. They're efficient because your vote truly has the potential to change the result.

Do Your Homework

Voting is important but it is only useful if you vote for the right person. If you don't know the candidates, it's important to invest a bit of time to look them over. In this day and age it is pretty easy to do this quickly. Do a search for them on Google and look at their university website. Their university website will often have a downloadable CV or a link to their private sites. It's helpful to see if they have a presence on Twitter and if they do, what they tweet. You'll want to be mindful of how to spot Woke participants (see Section 3.3.1) based on their academic backgrounds, their methodological approaches and the use of Woke overt (see Section 3.1.4) or crossover (see Section 2.3.2) words.

Coordinate with Allies

If you have allies (see Section 3.5), you can consult and coordinate with them about the candidates for a vote. Ask them what they know about the candidates. You can let them know what you find out in your research. You can distribute the background work on candidates between yourselves. Ideally, you will vote for the same candidates as this will increase the likelihood of a (non-woke) candidate getting elected.

3.3 Identifying Allies

The last section looked at general counter wokecraft strategies. This section is the first of a series looking at something critical for successful counter wokecraft; working collectively with allies. It is difficult for one person to counter concerted and sustained Woke advances, especially once the CSJ perspective becomes entrenched. The more allies there are on-side, the more people can be counted on to coordinate against Woke advances.

3.3.1 How to Identify Woke Participants

The first step to identifying allies is being able to identify those who are not allies, i.e. Woke participants. The ease with which Woke participants can be identified has a lot to do with the stage of entrenchment of the CSJ perspective. The more entrenched the perspective is, the more easily identifiable Woke participants will be. Here is a series of things to watch out for when identifying Woke participants. They are organized according to the degree to which they indicate whether a participant is Woke. I.e. the first are less discriminant in the detection of Woke adherents and the latter the most.

The use of Woke crossover words: the use of Woke crossover words (and pronouns, such as "they" instead of the 3rd person singular he or she) is common among Woke participants. Especially when the words are used in unusual ways, such as the addition of the word "critical" when it seems superfluous. Crossover words will be preferred to overt Woke words in early stage entrenchment. In this way, and in these circumstances, they are used partly to signal to other Woke participants and partly to lay the groundwork for the first Woke advances. The use of crossover words, while a pretty good Woke identifier, is not an instant tell. Crossover words are used intentionally because they can blend in and seem innocuous, so they won't necessarily be used with their Woke meaning, or by Woke participants.

Scepticism towards progress: An attitude of overt scepticism towards the notion of progress is characteristic of Woke participants. That things are better now than before is considered to be an Enlightenment notion used to hide the true oppressive nature of reality. Similar sentiments will be held for notions that environmental conditions are better than before. Watch also for disparaging and dismissive commentary on technology, electronics, etc. This is not perfectly discriminant since these attitudes can be shared both by the Woke proximate and the uninitiated.

Disciplinary background: This is the most easily observable characteristic for identifying Woke participants. Critical Social Justice is now the dominant intellectual perspective in the fine arts, humanities and social sciences.

Economics and some streams of philosophy, psychology and political science currently remain outside of its grip. That said, if a participant is from fine arts, the humanities or social sciences, there is a good chance they are Woke.

Methodological approach: Together with disciplinary background, methodological approach is a good indicator of whether a participant is likely to be Woke. Participants from the fine arts, humanities and social sciences whose work is non-quantitative or non-analytic are even more likely to be Woke than other members of their disciplines. This is particularly true if such participants come across as being sceptical towards quantitative approaches as well as to positivism more generally (i.e. the hypothetico-deductive method). If such scepticism is communicated sardonically or flippantly, this is a further indication that the participant is Woke.

Public demeanor: Woke participants are, for the most part, vocal and self-assured. This is related to the fervor of their belief in the Critical Social Justice perspective. The more vocal and self-assured they are about central CSJ concerns (e.g. EDI), the more likely they are to be Woke. They will tend to be more vocal and self-assured as the CSJ perspective becomes more entrenched (see Section 2.1.5).

The use of Woke projection: This is a technique where Woke participants will at once demonstrate adherence to the CSJ perspective from their own "position" while at the same time accusing, with an attempt to shame, others inhabiting the same position as them. A typical example of this would be the following. First, a white male participant would ostentatiously and publicly "recognize" their own privilege. Second, they would performatively make a claim or take an action that demonstrates their fealty to the CSJ perspective. They might say that because of their privilege they couldn't possibly provide their opinion on a given topic. The second part of this manoeuvre is also a projection of culpability onto other "white males" and a way to insinuate that they shouldn't provide their opinion about the issue either. This technique can also be considered a Woke bullying technique (see Section 2.4.2).

Overreaction to opposition: Woke participants are more likely to overreact if they encounter resistance to a woke advance. This can manifest itself through the display of unusual amounts of aggression towards an opponent, *ad hominem* attacks, threatening to leave or resign, or possibly even having what appears to be a tantrum if a woke advance is not successful.

The Use of overt Woke words: The use of overt Woke words (see Section 3.1.4) is the most discriminant indicator of a Woke participant. Non-Woke participants will not use such words and likely won't understand them or even know them. If someone uses them, they're almost certainly Woke. These words are least likely to be used in early stages of entrenchment, and most likely to be used in later stages (see Section 2.1.5). Their use in early entrenchment is an indicator of the fervently Woke. The only circumstance in which this is not the case is if a dissident is using such a word when trying to describe, or explain a concept of, the CSJ perspective.

3.3.2   Characteristics of Potential Allies

To be sure, given the current academic environment where any hint of questioning the CSJ perspective is vilified, potential allies can be difficult to spot. In many ways identifying potential allies is done in juxtaposition to the identification of Woke participants. While there are no hard and fast rules, here are five things to look out for when trying to identify potential allies.

Clear dissidents: There are some people who are fearless, oblivious, or simply combative Woke dissidents. They are knowledgeable about the CSJ perspective and will overtly oppose it. They are clearly potential allies. These people are rare.

Disciplinary background: This is the most obvious characteristic for identifying allies. As mentioned above, there are very few dissidents in the fine arts, humanities or social sciences. The main exception is economics. They can be found in psychology and political science too. There are more dissidents in STEM fields and most reliably (although they may be uninitiated, latent dissidents) in engineering. Scientific disciplines with an environmental vocation (e.g. climate, environmental science, etc.) will tend to have fewer dissidents and more who are sympathetic to CSJ, i.e. Woke proximate (see Section 1.6.2).

Methodological approach: The type of research matters a lot in identifying allies. Anyone adopting quantitative methods is more likely to be a potential ally. Again though, this is not always the case since quantitative scholars can also be Woke proximate.

Public demeanor: Dissidents, holding unpopular opinions are most likely to keep their opinions to themselves. As a result, people who rarely express themselves, particularly on issues central to the CSJ perspective (e.g. EDI) are potentially hidden allies.

Scholars who seem Woke, but don't use Woke words: This is a relatively small group of participants, but they can be powerful allies. These are participants in the fine arts, humanities or social sciences but who are not Woke. They may look Woke on the outside (apparel, hairstyle, etc.). They may even study topics cherished by the CSJ perspective (e.g. indigenous issues). They can be identified because they will not use Woke words in general, nor to describe their work, particularly words like "critical", "oppression," etc. They will self-describe their work in non-hyperbolic terms. These can be powerful allies because they will normally be very familiar with the CSJ perspective and understand it. If you're not very familiar with the CSJ perspective, they can help you to understand it yourself and to understand how to counter it.

3.3.3   Making Contact with Allies

Unfortunately, the above characteristics cannot guarantee that someone is an ally. To reliably identify an ally, it's necessary to make contact with them. This should be done to the extent possible one-on-one. This can be done in various ways, but the best is in person, over a meal or a drink. The purpose of the meeting can be justified as an attempt to see about potential collaboration or some other plausible pretense. It can also be done explicitly with the goal to discuss the Critical Social Justice perspective. The invitation to the meeting is best done in person or by phone, avoiding any electronic record. At the same time, in the current circumstances (COVID-19) it might be necessary to contact and meet with potential allies electronically.

The main goal of such a meeting is to establish whether or not the person is a potential ally. The question to be broached is whether the person is familiar with the Critical Social Justice perspective. If they are, you'll want to ask what they think of it. The answer to this question will let you know whether they are a potential ally. If they haven't heard of CSJ, you'll have to be prepared to describe it to them (see Section 1.2 on the CSJ worldview), ideally as objectively as possible. During this discussion you'll have to read (perhaps carefully) their responses for whether they are a likely ally.

3.4 From Contact to Working Together to Counter Wokecraft

This step is important since it is the only way to truly establish whether someone is a potential ally. It is also the best way to establish whether there is the potential to work with them to counter wokecraft. This section is about what you should do after contact is made.

3.4.1 Informing about the Critical Social Justice perspective

Allies can be divided between those who know about the CSJ perspective (dissidents) and those who don't (the uninitiated). If you've been able to identify uninitiated potential allies, you can think of them as latent dissidents (see Section 1.6.5). It will not be necessary to inform dissidents about the CSJ perspective, but it is important to do so for uninitiated latent dissidents. It's important because latent dissidents will likely be opposed instinctively to CSJ and in particular its prescriptions (e.g. hiring quotas based on identity). They'll find the prescriptions unfair and illogical, but they won't have the analytical tools to understand it, and they won't understand just what a threat the perspective represents; to the university, to science and to society. It's for these reasons that you'll need to inform them about the CSJ perspective.

Providing a lay-of-the-land of the CSJ perspective succinctly is important, as is emphasizing the implications of the perspective. Since most latent dissidents will be from STEM fields, it will be important to emphasize the implications of the CSJ perspective for science. A good place to start in terms of the lay-of-the-land is the three CSJ principles (see Section 1.2). You can also point latent dissidents to documentation that you have found useful to understand the CSJ perspective. In fact, they may explicitly ask for this. I find Cynical Theories Pluckrose and Lindsay (2020) to be the best one-stop-shop for this, but there are many resources available. The choice of resources to suggest can be delicate since to the uninitiated, resources can seem extreme and strident. You don't want to scare them off, so you'll have to use your judgement on the best source for a given person.

In terms of the implications of the perspective for science, a few things are particularly important. Namely, that according to the CSJ perspective:

- science cannot access the true nature of reality (i.e. it can't get at any truth about the world);
- science has no authority over any way of understanding the world (i.e. it's not any more reliable than religion or superstition);
- science is inherently and irredeemably racist;
- science was designed to perpetuate the oppression of white European males at the expense of everyone else; and
- the CSJ perspective is almost entirely theoretically derived - it's based on unfalsifiable assertion.

Most scientists will recognize the CSJ perspective for what it is, anti-science, anti-scientific, unfalsifiable doctrine; the exact thing science was developed to overcome. This is likely to sharpen their interest in opposing Woke incursions in universities, if not in science. It may not be possible to communicate all this in one meeting. It might take a few. For the uninitiated, these ideas are very foreign and can take a while to make sense and sink in. (I recently wrote an essay with this target audience in mind (Pincourt; 2021a).)

The motivation for recruiting allies is often punctual: an upcoming vote on a new hire in your department, say. Since it can take quite a while for these ideas to sink in, it's best to start the process of recruiting allies as long in advance as possible. It's also best not to rush this kind of recruitment, even if it means suffering a Woke incursion. Sometimes, of course, given the importance of the incursion, it may be necessary though.

3.4.2   Agreeing to Work Together

Once you feel comfortable that someone is an ally, the next step is to agree to work together. This doesn't need to be too formal, but it's important that it is agreed to explicitly. There are many ways in which dissidents can work together but in order for the collaboration to be effective, it requires at least two things:

Agree to support each other: This is pretty straightforward but effective. You'll need to agree that if your ally opposes a CSJ advance, you will support the opposition. This does not need to be very elaborate. Most of the time, it simply means publicly voicing agreement with your ally. This reduces the ability of Woke participants to exaggerate support for a given Woke advance. (One detail here: it's best not to be too overt about your collaboration. If you're in a meeting, for example, it's best not to sit together.)

Agree to defend each other: This also is pretty straightforward and effective. You'll need to agree that if someone criticizes your ally or their argument against a Woke advance, you'll defend them. Most of the time, this simply means publicly speaking out on behalf of your ally in this context. If your ally faces an *ad hominem* reproach, you can say that the reproach is unjustified and that your colleauge was simply expressing him- or herself. If the argument is criticized, you can try to rephrase it differently. This will reduce the ability of Woke participants to quell dissent during Woke advances.

3.5 Coordinating with Allies to Counter Wokecraft

The last section looked at how to go from making contact to agreeing to work with an ally. This section is about laying the groundwork to effectively counter wokecraft. This ultimately relies on coordinating with allies towards a number of different goals.

3.5.1 Recruiting Other Allies

An important task is to assemble like-minded participants as allies. This is more easily done the more allies there are since recruitment is easily distributed. It's best for this task to be done one-to-one. While it's possible to do it jointly with other dissidents, it can seem intimidating to a potential ally being approached. At the same time, it's a good idea to identify potential allies with confirmed allies since you will have more information at your disposal about the potential ally. Once identified, potential allies can be approached like you did with your first ally (see Section 3.3.3).

3.5.2 Identifying Sites of Intervention

Interventions take place in specific administrative situations where decisions are made; sites of intervention. You'll need to make a list of possible sites of intervention, or at least be conscious of them. They include departmental-, faculty- and university-wide committees and assemblies. Each of these is a possible site of intervention. This is best done with allies since different people are aware of different sites of intervention throughout the university.

3.5.3 Know the Terrain at the Site of Intervention

When considering different sites of intervention it's important to know who the participants are and (as closely as possible) how they will fall on Woke issues and advances, and if they will say anything. For the most part, participants can be divided between those who will support, or not oppose, Woke advances (the Woke and Woke-proximate) and those more likely to oppose them (dissidents and latent dissidents). Knowing this is useful to establish the dynamics at the sites of intervention and should be used in prioritizing them.

3.5.4 Prioritizing Interventions

It's good practice to counter wokecraft when you come across it. At the same time, not all situations involve a Woke threat, so that even if you were present, you would probably not come across anything that would need to be countered. Similarly, there are some sites where interventions can have little impact. Finally, you probably can't intervene everywhere. It's important therefore to prioritize (collaboratively if possible) where dissident interventions are likely to be most effective. Here are some things to keep in mind when prioritizing interventions.

- **Priority #1 - Faculty hiring:** Given that professors are around for a long time, and since they show up over their careers all through university administrations, they hold a great deal of power over the long term direction of the university. As a result, being involved at all stages of hiring (position description, hiring committee, etc.) is of the highest priority.

- **Don't get spread too thin:** The more allies you have, the more you can coordinate with, and the more situations you can intervene in. The fewer you have, the more judicious you have to be in choosing your interventions. Don't spread yourselves too thin. This is a question of human resources.

- **Prioritize situations with bigger impact:** In Section 3.2 on general counter-wokecraft I suggested you should aim as high up the chain as you can. Consistent with this, you should prioritize situations that will have more impact. I.e. at the faculty-level rather than at the department level, the university level rather than the faculty, etc. This needs to be nuanced in some circumstances, since for example, some decisions are less likely to be turned down the further up in the administration something goes. This is the case for proposed new faculty hires. For new faculty hires, the most important site of intervention is the department.

- **Prioritize academic administrative search committees:** Since academic administrators have a big impact on the direction universities take, and since the appointment processes commonly invite faculty participation, they are accessible high-impact opportunities.

- **Prioritize situations where you can make a difference:** If a given situation has only Woke representation, it may be fruitless to intervene there. You can have the most impact in situations where there is some Woke representation, but where Woke representation is not hegemonic.

3.5.5 Ensuring Dissident Representation

Identifying sites of intervention means identifying sites where it's useful to have a dissident presence. As a result, once sites are identified, the aim is to ensure dissident representation. If it turns out that there is already dissident representation, this might not be necessary. If there is no dissident representation, or if there is not enough, the aim is to ensure there is. This can be done in a few ways.

The dissident representation can be you or other dissident allies. If you want to represent the dissident voice, you can volunteer yourself. This is usually straightforward and more often than not this will be accepted. It may require a bit of digging to figure out to whom the request needs to be made. In other cases, appointment to committees (say for the selection of a dean) can require a formal vote. If you want to be on such a committee, coordinate with allies so that they vote for you. Appointment to such positions often relies on only a few votes, even those at the faculty or university-wide level.

If you don't want, or are unable, to be on a given high-priority committee, coordinate with allies to ensure that dissidents are represented. You and your allies can coordinate to suggest dissidents as members of committees. You can also vote for, and encourage others to vote for dissidents as well.

3.5.6 Limiting Representation of Woke Participants

Ensuring dissident representation will, for the most part, reduce Woke representation. It is also a good idea to work explicitly to reduce Woke representation. This can be done by discouraging the inclusion of Woke participants in circumstances in which you or Woke allies can have an influence. Woke participants will typically try to recruit Woke allies. If they try, you should argue against the inclusion of such participants, and you should always have an alternative to propose. Even if they don't try, if new or additional participants are required for any given situation, always have a dissident candidate to propose (see Section 3.2.3) and be ready to argue for their inclusion. Should a Woke participant threaten to make a dramatic departure (see Section 2.4.5), this opportunity to limit representation should be taken. Acceptance of the departure should be made earnestly while expressing gratitude for the departing participant's contribution. If appropriate, compensation such as severance can be offered. In the aftermath of the departure, there may be attempts to use it as evidence for the oppressive nature of the environment at the site and to unsettle or disrupt it. This should be opposed by arguing the departure is nothing more than the frustration of one individual.

3.6 Sowing Doubt about the Critical Social Justice Perspective

As you and your allies begin to work together, one of the most useful things you can do is sow doubt about the CSJ perspective among colleagues.

The Critical Social Justice movement is characterized by extreme moral confidence; confidence that the perspective is unassailably true, right and just. There is little chance of convincing the Woke otherwise. This is not the case for latent dissidents, the Woke proximate or the uninitiated more generally, however. Some of these people will be sceptical about the CSJ perspective, but won't know why. Others will be sympathetic to notions of social justice and might even use Woke words and terms, despite not really understanding them. In particular, they might not see or appreciate the retributive, anti-liberal, extreme egalitarianism of the CSJ perspective. If these people can be shown what this worldview implies, their willingness to accept the perspective can be compromised and/or their doubts amplified. This is one reason that it's important to say something when you see something; it can sow doubt in those who may never otherwise hear criticisms of the CSJ perspective. While there are different lines of argument that can be used, it's a good idea to first try to disarm any situation in which you are trying to sow doubt.

3.6.1 Disarming the Situation

It is common when trying to sow doubt among the Woke proximate and uninitiated to launch directly into arguments against the CSJ perspective. The problem with this approach is that given the current climate, people will often react badly to any criticism whatsoever of the perspective. Very quickly, people can think, even without understanding why, that any criticism you bring up implies that you are right-wing, a racist, a white supremacist or any other negative epithet that might spring to mind.

As a result, it is important to begin the presentation of any criticism with one or two disarming introductory statements and a disarming tone. Naturally, you need to believe the statements and you should avoid using Woke words (see Section 3.1.4 on Woke words). It is also helpful to demonstrate sympathy with the particular cause under discussion as well as camaraderie with your interlocutor. This can be done by starting simply with a statement such as "Like you, I don't think anyone should be discriminated against based on X [e.g. skin color, sex, etc.]. At the same time, what concerns me about Y [the critical social justice perspective, Critical Race Theory, EDI, etc.] is..." This increases the chance that the discussion will get off on the right foot and that you'll be able to successfully sow doubt. Once you've done this, you can continue with some common lines of argument.

3.6.2 Equality of Opportunity vs. Outcome

One line of argument is to express concern about the distinction between equality of opportunity and equality of outcome. Equality of opportunity is an ultimate goal of traditional liberalism, and one for which the Civil Rights movement was successfully fought. It means that nobody should be prevented from pursuing what they would like to do in life as a result of sex, skin color, gender, sexual orientation, religious belief, etc. In other words, all people should be evaluated based on their merits. That all people should be treated thus is known as "universalism." This does not mean that everyone will be a doctor, but it means that no one capable should be prevented from being a doctor as a result of their skin color, sex, sexual orientation, etc.

The CSJ perspective on the other hand advocates for equality of outcome based on identity, i.e. equity. This is because according to the CSJ perspective, any difference in outcome observable according to identity is the result of bigotry. As such, the perspective advocates for the intentional promotion of some ("historically oppressed") identities over others, as well as advocating for implicit and explicit discrimination against other (historically oppressor) identities. In the words of the most frequently cited Critical Race Theorist, Ibram X. Kendi "The only remedy to past discrimination is present discrimination. The only remedy to present discrimination is future discrimination"(Kendi; 2019). The types of discrimination typically advocated for are quotas or lowered objective standards of evaluation for target identities. Such discrimination is also often framed as being justified in order to "redress" historical injustices and implies holding contemporary members of "oppressor identities" responsible for injustices perpetuated by other people. There are a number of reasons for which concern can be expressed with this extreme egalitarian ethic.

3.6.3   Equity is Too Simplistic

The notion of equity is extremely simplistic. Many factors influence outcomes in life. Assuming that *any* differences in outcome are the result of bigotry is to attribute far too many factors into one coarse and blunt explanation. Ultimately this can be thought of as an "equity trick" that amounts to measuring equality of opportunity with equality of outcome.

3.6.4   The CSJ Perspective is Discriminatory

Naturally, distribution of resources according to identity is by definition discriminatory. If it is done on the basis of skin color, or "race" it is itself racist. It is for this reason that Critical Social Justice is increasingly referred to as "neo-racist." If it is done on the base of sex, it is itself sexist, etc.

3.6.5   Inclusion Begets Exclusion

While inclusion is a nice sounding word, the reality is that "inclusion" that results in the distribution of resources according to identity, automatically implies distributing fewer resources to all other identities. Inclusion therefore implies exclusion. Inclusion can also serve as justification for removal or purging of identities considered as "oppressors" or over-represented.

3.6.6   Bad Historical Track Record

It's useful to point out that there are many historical examples of discrimination according to group identity, and that these examples have been disastrous. The examples are myriad, but the death of hundreds of millions in the Soviet Union and Communist China, not to mention the Jewish Holocaust represent a few horrific examples. Finally, it can be explained that such atrocities are typically justified as morally righteous at first and often turn gruesome quickly, if not unexpectedly.

3.6.7 Two Wrongs Don't Make a Right

Such discrimination is advocated for in order to right historical wrongs. While this sounds virtuous, it clearly flies in the face of the most basic notions of justice that we teach even to children. We teach this to children because we understand the risk of the escalation of conflict and injustice.

3.6.8 The Antithesis of the Golden Rule

The Golden Rule is a maxim of most religions and cultures and is the principle that one should treat others as one expects to be treated themselves. Distributing resources on the basis of identity is clearly antithetical to this rule. It is also interesting to note that this maxim, according to the CSJ perspective, could be seen merely as a rule originating from oppressive Western culture whose aim is ultimately to further perpetuate oppressive Western power structures. The fact that this maxim is found in most religions of the world is clear evidence that such a claim is spurious.

3.6.9 Restricting Candidate Pools Risks Lowering Standards

Hiring with quotas necessarily reduces the size of applicant pools. This necessarily reduces the chances of finding the best candidate. This has nothing to do with the quality of the candidates targeted with the quota. It is simply statistical; as the applicant pool decreases, the chances of finding the best candidate decrease.

3.6.10 Runs Risk of Perpetuating Discrimination

Hiring by quota, by positive discrimination or affirmative action increases the likelihood that people will doubt the qualifications of the people hired. This can lead to people saying things like "X was hired only because they were Y-identity." This can have the opposite effect desired and prove caustic in a professional setting.

3.6.11 Undermining the Self-confidence of Qualified "Diverse" Candidates

An unintended consequence of distributing resources according to identity can be to undermine the confidence of candidates selected based on ability or merit, but who are members of "designated" identities. Such candidates can worry about the legitimacy of their position and even be affected by impostor syndrome as they suffer tremendous doubt about whether they were selected merely based on their identity.

3.6.12 Penalizing an Individual for Group Membership

Penalizing an individual for actions perpetuated by others who share the same identity is obviously discriminatory. As important, however, is that it flies in the face of the liberal tradition recognizing individual rights, freedoms and responsibilities; that individuals are accountable for their own actions and not those of others, even those who share the same identity with them.

3.6.13 CSJ is Anti-real, Anti-science and Anti-scientific

This line of argumentation is most effective with people from the sciences, although it can be useful to others as well. I covered this in Section 3.4.1 on making contact with potential allies, so I won't belabor it here. That said, it's worth communicating to people not familiar with the CSJ perspective what the perspective itself implies about knowledge and what we can know. This is most extreme when one considers the perspective's implications for science.

In particular, the CSJ perspective is sceptical towards the authority of science as a way of knowing about reality. That is, it is claimed that science cannot know about the nature of reality and that science has no more authority about the nature of reality than religion or superstition. It is just one "story" among many about reality. Moreover, because science was developed primarily by white male Europeans, it is considered inherently and irredeemably racist. This, it is claimed, is because science was designed to advantage its developers to the detriment of those they wanted to subjugate and oppress. As a result, the CSJ perspective actively seeks to discredit and overthrow science (see my essay on this in Merion-West (Pincourt; 2021a)). Finally, all these claims about science are almost entirely theoretical. They are based on assertion and interpreted as doctrine.

3.6.14 How to Go about Sowing Doubt

Doubt can be sown in at least a couple different contexts. One context is the one described in Section 3.3 on identifying allies. This is probably the best context to sow doubt. It involves meeting with people one-on-one over a meal or a drink. Doubt can also be sown during the course of meetings and can be integrated with saying something when you see something (see Section 3.2.1). This context is a little bit less controlled, and since other things need to be resolved during a meeting, sowing doubt can be interrupted, less effective and less predictable.

3.7   Formalizing Meetings

A key tactic by Woke participants for making CSJ advances in universities is to insist on informality in general, and in decision-making meetings in particular (see Section 2.4.1). This results in meetings having little structure and informal decision making. Informality is exploited by Woke participants in a number of ways. They can take over the agenda. This can be done to surprise people and have things passed with little or insufficient reflection. They can add items for discussion to filibuster and prevent other things (which they don't like) from being discussed and delay them. Finally, informality can be exploited to bully, intimidate and force through decisions which they favor. Enmity towards secret ballot voting for example and insisting on "consensus" all force people's hands and discourage dissent. As a result, it is important to short-circuit the possibility of such tactics. Ensuring formality in meetings is key to doing this. There are a number of things that can be done to formalize meetings to protect from wokecraft.

3.7.1   Volunteer to Chair Meetings

If it is possible, the best way to be able to insist on formality in meetings is to chair them yourself. Often these will be meetings you will have to attend in any case, so chairing them involves little additional responsibility.

3.7.2   Ensure Voting Procedures are in Place

There should be formalized rules for decision making and as much as possible, decisions should be made by (secret ballot) vote. If you are chair, you can put things to vote. Don't be afraid to do so even if people object. If you aren't the chair, you should ask the chair to have appropriate decisions go to vote. (See Section 3.9 for more on Secret Ballot Voting.)

3.7.3   Ensure There is an Agenda

To avoid surprise items, it is crucial to have an agenda[6] for a meeting. If you are chairing a meeting you can ensure there is one. If you are not, ask the chair to provide one.

3.7.4   Establish the Agenda beforehand

If you are chairing the meeting, draft the agenda yourself. You should circulate it beforehand and ask for input. It's good to provide a deadline for adding items to the agenda. It's also good to have an "Other Business" agenda item. This is useful in case people try to add items at the last minute. Any items proposed after the deadline should be covered in "Other Business." If you are not chairing the meeting, ask for an agenda from the chair as long before the meeting as possible/reasonable. The important thing is having the agenda beforehand.

3.7.5   Assign Times to Agenda Items

To prevent filibustering, it's important that each item have an assigned amount of time for discussion. The amount of time for an item should allow sufficient discussion, but the amount of time assigned for an item should not be surpassed. If time is running out, participants should be reminded of this. If you are the chair, you can assign times to each item. If you are not, ask the chair to add them. You can propose times for each item to the chair.

3.7.6   Stick to the Agenda

Agenda items and the times associated with them should be adhered to. If they are not, Woke participates will be able to claim that the time was not adhered to before, and insist that it not be when they desire.

---

[6]You can download an example agenda at https://woke-dissident.github.io/images/agenda.pdf

3.7.7   Close, Decide or Table

At the end of the time allotted to an item, one of three things should be done. If it was only an informational item, discussion should be closed. If the item requires a decision, a decision should be made or the item should be tabled for another meeting. Decisions should be made by a formal (secret ballot) vote (see Section 3.9). Additional discussion should be discouraged. If someone insists on extending discussion, the extension should be considered a motion and be voted on.

3.7.8   Identify Relevant Documents in Agenda

Make sure that any documents relevant to discussions be identified in the agenda. The same deadline for adding items should be used for relevant documents. Relevant documents should be circulated along with the agenda.

3.7.9   Recording and Circulating Minutes

It's very important, once a meeting is done to have meeting minutes. Particularly important is having decisions recorded and ideally, associated discussion will also be recorded. If you are the chair, to ensure an accurate recording of information, it's best for you (or an ally) to draft the minutes. It's best to produce and circulate them shortly (within a day or so) after the meeting. Avoid allowing Woke participants draft them. If you are not the chair, ask for the minutes from the chair. If you receive them, review them and ask for changes if they do not reflect your understanding of the meeting. You can of course also volunteer to draft them.

3.8   Strategies to Facilitate Dissent from Wokecraft

There are three broad categories of Woke tactics: subterfuge, exaggerating support and quelling dissent (see Section 2.5). Tactics that quell dissent discourage people from providing their opinions on, or from opposing, Woke advances. Most of them revolve around intimidation. In this section I discuss two tactics that can be used to counter the quelling of dissent in the context of meetings.

3.8.1   Allowing Anonymous Input

Woke ethics, extreme moral self-righteousness and bullying tactics can make it very uncomfortable for people to challenge or oppose Woke advances, no matter how small, well-intentioned, or well-defended the opposition may be. A common reaction to this is for people simply not to say anything. One tactic to oppose this and encourage the voicing of opinions is to allow people the opportunity to provide input anonymously. There are various options for this. If you are chairing a meeting, you should try to incorporate them. If you are not, you should ask the chair to do so.

Suggestion Boxes

This is a low-tech, asynchronous method requiring a bit of organization. This can work well if agendas are distributed before meetings. This allows people to know what will be discussed and to submit any comments beforehand. The suggestions can be brought up by the chair during the meeting.

Electronic Audience Interaction

COVID moved many things online and habituated people to electronic participation in meetings. Services like "slido"[7] can make this very easy. Moreover, they can allow anonymous participation. It's important to remember that such approaches can be used in-person as well.

---

[7]https://www.sli.do/

Secret Ballot Voting

The same reasons justifying the importance of allowing anonymous input apply for secret ballot voting. Secret Ballot Voting (SBV), however, is even more important since it is through votes (formal or informal) that decisions are actually made. As a result, Secret Ballot Voting is the single most important initiative that can be used to enable dissent. The key for SBV to work is to ensure that decision-making is formalized through votes, and that it is impossible for anyone to know how anyone else votes. I outline good practice for Secret Ballot Voting in a section (Section 3.9) dedicated to it below. As with anonymous input, there are two main options. If you are chairing a meeting, you should try to incorporate them. If you are not, you should ask the chair to do so.

- **Pen-and-paper ballots:** This is low-tech. It can be synchronous (done in real-time), but is easier to manage asynchronously.

- **Electronic voting:** Since COVID and the increase in online meetings there are evermore options to facilitate this. Zoom for example has built-in SBV that can be used during a meeting. It can be parametrized so that neither participants nor the host knows how anyone votes. There are also all kinds of other asynchronous online voting options such as electionrunner.[8] Some of these services are free while others are paid. There's lots of information to help you decide which is best for you.[9]

3.9   Secret Ballot Voting to Counter Wokecraft

It's important to see that when group decisions are made at universities, they are almost always done explicitly or implicitly by vote. In the majority of situations votes are undertaken informally. Moreover, since even

---

[8]https://electionrunner.com/
[9]See e.g. https://www.capterra.com/voting-software/

academics tend to avoid conflict, Woke advances are made in a three-part process. Proposal, support, acceptance. In other words, a Woke advance is proposed. This is then supported (typically accompanied by a good dose of high-minded moral rhetoric) by at least one other Woke participant.

Key to this process is that non-Woke participants will often not say anything. This is partly because of a climate of general Woke intimidation (see Section 2.4.2) and partly because the non-Woke will often justify to themselves that the advance is minor and will be insignificant in the long-term. In the end, Woke participants will agree that consensus has been achieved and that the proposal has been accepted unanimously. The proposal is then passed. In circumstances where Woke participants are not in the majority, the secret ballot vote is the key to breaking this cycle. It prevents Woke participants from being able to intimidate other participants and preventing them from opposing their advances. That's why Woke participants are so opposed to secret ballot voting. Importantly, secret ballots are also the key to making sure the Woke don't become the majority. It's for this reason that it is essential to institute secret ballot voting.

3.9.1   Secret Ballot Voting Ideals

Secret ballot voting exists for some circumstances at all universities. SBV is typically reserved for "more important" decisions. Sometimes it is institutionalized for particular decisions through collective agreements or university policy. On balance, there are however, few decisions that are made by SBV, although many through informal votes. There are two dimensions along which Secret Ballot Voting can be characterized and which help to understand ideal secret ballot voting. How votes are triggered, and what decisions require a vote.

- **Non-discretionary triggers:** Ideally, the circumstances under which decisions are submitted to secret ballot should be formalized (written down) and be non-discretionary. If they are discretionary so that they are, for example, triggered by a request, Woke intimidation will cause a "chill" on secret ballots. As a result, it is good to have explicit rules that govern when secret ballots are used.

84

- **As broad as possible:** Ideally, as many decisions as possible should be submitted to secret ballot. This will ensure the greatest amount of resilience in your institution.

3.9.2 How to Institute Secret Ballot Voting

Instituting broad, non-discretionary secret ballot voting is not always easy but it will pay off in the long run. To institute it requires both an offence and a defense. The offence requires instilling a culture of secret ballot voting. The defense requires responding to resistance.

Instilling a Culture of Secret Ballot Voting

Instituting secret ballot voting can be straightforward, but it can also encounter resistance from the Woke and non-Woke alike. As a result it is necessary to carefully evaluate how to instill a culture of secret ballot voting. The best, although longer-term way, is incrementally. If you're the chair of a decision-making body you can introduce secret ballot voting in the decision-making process. (This is another good reason to be chair.) If you're not, you can ask the chair to do so for given types of decisions. It is good to start with non-controversial decisions with low stakes. Having these initial votes will habituate people to the process and allow you to figure out how best to organize them. (There are various ways to organize them as I described in Section 3.9.) Once people begin to get used to it, you can then try to formalize secret ballot procedures. The idea is for voting to be incrementally adopted with clear, non-discretionary triggers covering the broadest range of decisions possible over time.

Prepare for Resistance

The reasons for resistance to secret ballot voting will be different for different types of participants. You should be prepared for this. The first thing is to be able to explain the advantages of secret ballot voting.

Explaining Why SBV is Important

The best argument for secret ballot voting (which is also true) is that secret ballot voting enables people who are reluctant (or intimidated) to voice
opinions or concerns to have a say in decision-making. This can be justified
for junior faculty, for example, who could be worried about tenure implications of expressing themselves on issues publicly. It turns out that SBV
is also advocated to enable "historically oppressed" minorities to have a say
in decision-making. Ultimately it allows everyone to have a say in decision-
making and is the basis of democracy. This can be added as a response to
any criticism, e.g. "Isn't it worth X to ensure everybody's voice is heard?"

Have Answers for Common Criticisms

In addition to explaining its advantages, you'll want to have answers ready
for common criticisms likely to be raised against secret ballot voting.

It's too cumbersome: This is most likely to be raised by non-Woke participants. You can answer by saying that a little more time is worth ensuring that everyone's voice is counted. With the increasing availability of synchronous and asynchronous electronic voting, this argument is basically ob-
solete.

It cuts off discussion: This argument is fallacious but will be used. One
way to respond is to say that ample time will be allocated to discussion (it
is important to build time into agendas for discussion so that this claim is
true). Moreover, you can say that to encourage and feed discussion anonymous electronic methods like "slido"[10] can and should be used. This rein-
forces the need for the availability of anonymity as well as encouraging more
discussion. Finally, you can say that discussion needs to end at some point
for a decision to be made.

It's too divisive: I confess to not really understanding this criticism, but

---

[10]https://www.sli.do/

I have heard it. The best response is simply to ask the critic to consider whether it is not more divisive that some people feel like their voice can't be heard.

It is a master's tool: This criticism tries to delegitimize SBV with Critical Social Justice theory by maintaining that since SBV was developed in Western Civilization that it is inherently racist, sexist, etc. This argument is also fallacious. A very lengthy response could be made involving many arguments mentioned throughout this manual. Perhaps the best is simply to say that SBV is the keystone of our democracies and has enabled the peaceful, prosperous societies we live in.

It's too binary: This is also a CSJ-inspired response. It implies that categorization (in this case between "yes" and "no") is an exercise of power and as a result unjust. The simplest response to this is that at some point a binary decision will have to be made and that SBV is the best to ensure that everyone's voice is heard.

There are other decision-making traditions that can be used: This typically involves a criticism of Western methods of decision-making as being too confrontational and that methods from other (non-Western) cultures can be used. These methods typically involve different ways of eliciting input and discussion. To respond to this criticism you can say there is nothing preventing these methods from being incorporated, but in the end a decision needs to be made and that SBV is the best for ensuring that everyone's voice is heard (I'm sounding like a broken record here!).

3.10 Making Sure Secret Ballot Votes are Transparent, Free and Fair

In order for Secret Ballot Voting to be effective in countering wokecraft, it needs to be transparent, free and fair. That it is transparent means the rules for how voting is to take place should be well defined and known beforehand. That it is free implies that people have to be able vote as they wish. Their vote must not be influenced by how anyone else wants them to vote. In order to ensure they are free therefore, people need to feel confident that their vote is truly anonymous. That they are fair means that protocols are followed and neither voting nor results can be manipulated. When necessary and practical, it is important that there be an election officer to handle voting, result compilation and reporting.

3.10.1   Voting Protocols

Having voting protocols means having rules for when and how votes are triggered, who can vote and how votes are organized. It is best for protocols to be written down and formally accepted.

3.10.2   Voting Triggers

As a general rule, votes should be triggered automatically so that they are not subject to voting chill or suppression. Voting chill and suppression can take place if intimidation is used to prevent formal, secret ballot votes from taking place. It's also good that triggers be designed to allow more than fewer votes. The more votes done by secret ballot, the more resilient your institution will be to wokecraft.

3.10.3   Eligible Voters

For any given situation, the list of eligible voters should be known beforehand. This will vary from context to context, but the important thing is for the universe of voters to be pre-defined. In some circumstances, only the votes of faculty will be eligible, in others student or staff representatives may also be eligible. Sometimes only those present in a given situation (e.g. departmental meeting) will be eligible, and sometimes status is sufficient (e.g. professor). The universe of eligible voters should not be too flexible so that it can be manipulated disingenuously or so that it can be difficult to establish voting eligibility (e.g. the sudden arrival of many unexpected participants demanding a vote).

3.10.4   Voting Organization

A key aspect of voting organization is to have an election officer whenever possible. Ideally the election officer will be independent of the decision being made. This is not always possible, and with advances in technology is increasingly unnecessary. Voting organization is highly influenced by the technological options available.

Electronic voting: Electronic voting can be done synchronously (e.g. in Zoom) or asynchronously (e.g. electionrunner[11]). Electronic options that allow for anonymous voting should always be used. Similarly, options announcing results (instead of having to go through an intermediary such as a chair), should also always be used.

Paper and pencil voting: When paper and pencil voting is used, various options are available. Of course, the best options are those that ensure anonymity and reduce the possibility of vote manipulation. In terms of anonymity, the best option is dual envelope voting. In this case, each eligible voter receives a ballot, and two envelopes. Ballots should be designed to require only a check mark or "X" and shouldn't require any handwriting. Ballots are placed by each voter into an anonymous envelope. The anonymous envelope is then placed into a second envelope that has the voter's printed name and their signature across the seal.

The best practice when compiling votes is to do so publicly and during the meeting or assembly. First, it needs to be established that all signed envelopes are from eligible voters. These envelopes are then opened and the anonymous envelopes set aside. Finally, the anonymous envelopes are opened and tallied. Make sure that necessary ballots and envelopes are prepared and available beforehand. If public tallying of votes is not used or

---

[11]https://electionrunner.com/

possible, it is best that this task be assigned to the election officer and that voting members be allowed to attend the tallying of the votes.

Fixed deadlines for asynchronous voting: If asynchronous voting is to be used it is important to define a deadline for when votes can be received and that votes arriving after the deadline will not be counted.

3.11   How to Win A Vote

This section looks at how to maximize the probability that votes will protect against wokecraft. Ultimately, this boils down to ensuring that decisions go to a formal (secret ballot) vote, and that you have the majority of votes. The context of this section is preventing an attempted Woke advance when a collective decision is being made (e.g. at a departmental meeting). It can also be used to institute decisions or policies to thwart future Woke advances.

Make sure a voting protocol is in place: Since most decisions at universities are made formally or informally by vote, it's important to make sure that a (secret ballot) voting protocol is in place (see section 3.9). This will ensure that when a final decision, is made, it will be done by vote. With a secret ballot vote, Woke participants will not be able to intimidate other participants to vote a given way (see Section 3.10 above).

Know who will be there and how they'll vote: It's good to know ahead of time, as best as possible, how people are likely to vote. This is useful mostly to help allocate resources. If there is little likelihood that a vote will support a Woke advance, there's no need to intervene. If a vote on a Woke advance is likely to be close, it might be possible to intervene to ensure an outcome against a Woke advance. To evaluate the direction of the vote, you might have to do some legwork. For the Woke and dissidents you will have a strong sense of how they will vote. For others, this may be less obvious. It is good practice to discuss the issue with those whose opinions seem uncertain about the vote to get a sense of how they are likely to vote.

Engage fence-sitters: If a vote will be close, to maximize the chance that an advance won't pass, you can engage with people who appear to be undecided. This can go hand-in-hand with making contact with a potential ally. The idea is for you to explain the advance in its broader Woke context. This will require giving a summary of the Woke worldview (see Section 1.2) and how the advance in question is an attempt entrench or further entrench that worldview.

Rally the troops: For close votes, you'll want to make sure allies and people likely to vote against a Woke advance know about the vote and encourage them to be present.

Work to Always Be the Majority: This is a longer term strategy and ties in with ensuring dissident representation (see Section 3.5.5). The idea is to ensure that as many decision-making venues have a majority of allies in place and are thereby able to vote against wokecraft.

Conclusion

When I began this project, I thought it would be faster to get to this stage; the stage of having a manual against wokecraft. Despite it taking longer than I imagined, I've covered the topics I intended to cover when I started. I plan to update the manual, hopefully with input from Woke dissidents who read it and find it useful, over time.

As I have learned more about Critical Social Justice in the process of writing the posts assembled into this manual, I've come to realize just how deep the roots of Critical Social Justice are in our universities. When I began, I saw the emergence of the Critical Social Justice perspective in our universities as a relatively sudden and recent phenomenon.

Of course, I was aware of what I thought were the primary precursors of the perspective from my undergraduate years in the 1990s. As such, as I began the project, I thought that the 1990s represented the birth of the perspective and its movement. As I learned more, however, its roots just kept stretching further and further back. I now recognize that those roots are very deep indeed. The earliest roots rest at least with the Greek skeptics and then with Rousseau and his romantic launching of the counter-enlightenment. That tradition carried on largely in Europe through Kant, Hegel and Nietzsche and up until the post-structuralists most commonly associated with "The Perspective."

I've come to see, however, that the Critical Social Justice perspective issued from the marriage of this eventually nihilistic tradition and a more goal-

93

oriented tradition emerging with Marx and brought to us through the Neo-Marxist Critical Theorists. The post-structuralists brought the artillery and the Critical Theorists the ethos. The rejoining of these traditions at the end of the 1980s crystallized the perspective and catalyzed the movement we now call Woke.

The Christmas before the publication of this manual, I read Allan Bloom's *The Closing of the American Mind*. It showed me that while I attributed the origins of the movement to the early 1990s, he had seen the same movement in the 1960s, and indeed that that movement had its own precursors the generation before. Trying to make sense of all these streams and torrents and fissures and roots, I can't help but think that our times are most directly the outcome Gramsci's blueprint for the disruption and co-opting of our institutions.

It's for this reason that I believe we need to recognize that the state of our universities is not the result of 2020 (Black Lives Matter) or Political Correctness (1990) or Berkeley (1960s), but most consistently Gramsci and his *Prison Notebooks* (1930s).

I bring this up to emphasize that this movement has a head start on us. We who want to bring universities back towards a liberal, universal, Enlightenment mission have witnessed a long-term effort to hijack the university and make it the handmaiden of an anti-liberal, anti-science moral activism. As a result, we mustn't imagine that righting the ship of the modern university will be done quickly. At the same time, it can be done, although it will have to be done as part of a concerted long term effort. I hope this manual, by explaining the worldview that has become so influential in our universities, the tactics used to gain control over them, and most importantly how those tactics can be demasked, defused and overturned will serve as part of the long march to bring universities back to their mission of knowledge and truth.

Bibliography

Abbot, D. S. (2017). "More weight": An academic's guide to surviving campus witch hunts.
URL: *https://quillette.com/2021/02/05/more-weight-an-academics-guide-to-surviving-campus-witch-hunts/*

Bahro, R. (1984). *From red to green: interviews with New Left Review*, Verso.

Barthes, R. (1968). La mort de l'auteur, *Manteia* **5**: 12–17.

Best, S. (1991). *Postmodern theory: Critical interrogations*, Macmillan International Higher Education.

Bloom, A. (2012). *The Closing of the American Mind: How Higher Education Has Failed Democracy and Impoverished the Souls of Today's Students*, 25th anniversary edn, New Dimensions Foundation.

Bookchin, M. (1982). *The ecology of freedom*, New Dimensions Foundation.

Carson, R. (2002). *Silent spring*, Houghton Mifflin Harcourt.

Crenshaw, K. (1990). Mapping the margins: Intersectionality, identity politics, and violence against women of color, *Stan. L. Rev.* **43**: 1241.

Domingos, P. (2021). Beating back cancel culture: A case study from the field of artificial intelligence.
URL: *https://quillette.com/2021/01/27/beating-back-cancel-culture-a-case-study-from-the-field-of-artificial-intelligence/*

Fahs, B. and Karger, M. (2016). Women's studies as virus: Institutional feminism, affect, and the projection of danger., *Multidisciplinary Journal of Gender Studies* **5**(1): 929–957.

Freudenrich, C. and Kiger, P. J. (2020). How viruses work.
URL: *https://science.howstuffworks.com/life/cellular-microscopic/virus-human1.htm*

Gutiérrez, R. (2017). Why mathematics (education) was late to the backlash party: The need for a revolution, *Journal of Urban Mathematics Education* **10**(2).

Haidt, J. (2012). *The righteous mind: Why good people are divided by politics and religion*, Vintage.

Hicks, S. R. C. (2011). *Explaining postmodernism: Skepticism and socialism from Rousseau to Foucault*, expanded edn, Ockham's Razor Publishing.

Kay, B. (2020). Learn from the best while you can.
URL: *https://nationalpost.com/opinion/barbara-kay-learn-from-the-best-while-you-can*

Kendi, I. X. (2019). *How to be an antiracist*, One world, New York.

Levin, Y. (2013). *The great debate: Edmund Burke, Thomas Paine, and the birth of right and left*, Basic Books (AZ).

Lindsay, J. (2020a). Critical theories: A virus on a liberal body politic.
URL: *https://newdiscourses.com/2020/03/critical-theories-virus-liberal-body-politic/*

Lindsay, J. (2020b). How the woke virus infects academia and our covid-19 response.
URL: *https://newdiscourses.com/2020/04/woke-virus-infects-academia-covid-19-response/*

Lundberg, C. O. and Keith, W. M. (2008). *The essential guide to rhetoric*, 2nd edn, Macmillan.

Pincourt, C. (2021a). DEI: a trojan horse for critical social justice in science.
URL: *https://merionwest.com/2021/04/08/dei-a-trojan-horse-for-critical-social-justice-in-science/*

Pincourt, C. (2021b). The subject principle in critical social justice thought.
URL: *https://areomagazine.com/2021/03/17/the-subject-principle-in-critical-social-justice-thought/*

Pluckrose, H. and Lindsay, J. A. (2020). *Cynical Theories: How Activist Scholarship Made Everything about Race, Gender, and Identity—and Why This Harms Everybody*, Pitchstone Publishing (US&CA).

Shackel, N. (2005). The vacuity of postmodernist methodology, *Metaphilosophy* **36**(3): 295–320.

Made in the USA
Las Vegas, NV
19 November 2021